Pearls of Hope

Pearls of Hope

A Forty-Day Devotional

Regina McIntosh

Foreword by Colette M. Blankenship

RESOURCE *Publications* · Eugene, Oregon

PEARLS OF HOPE
A Forty-Day Devotional

Resource Publications
An Imprint of Wipf and Stock Publishers
199 W. 8th Ave., Suite 3
Eugene, OR 97401

www.wipfandstock.com

PAPERBACK ISBN: 979-8-3852-3807-1
HARDCOVER ISBN: 979-8-3852-3808-8
EBOOK ISBN: 979-8-3852-3809-5

03/11/25

*For all the pearls who have graced
my life, my heart, my soul—
Jesus the King, my family and friends,
the ones who taught me to always hope*

Contents

Contents

Foreword

Romans 15:13 Now the God of hope fill you with all joy and peace in believing, that ye may abound in hope, through the power of the Holy Ghost.

I couldn't write a love letter to my husband without adding the word hope to it. "I hope you have a great day at work," "I hope you get home early tonight," "I hope we have time together this evening," etc. etc. Hope is such a strong, powerful word. A word we use in our communication with one another, every day. Hope is also a important part of what we're feeling.

There have been so many time during my 41 years of life when I truly believed that I was about to lose hope. I felt like giving up, felt like what I was struggling with would never end, like things wouldn't get any better for me or my family. But God . . . He has always proved me wrong! And, for that, I am so thankful.

Finally, I am filled with hope because of the One who came to bring love like hearts could never comprehend without the sacrifice, the Son, Jesus, who taught us that He would always bring hope beyond words, hope that we can't even begin to describe, hope that fulfills our heart's yearning for life eternal. Jesus is our hope!

God has proved that I am wise to feel so assured of this hope and one more reason I feel so hopeful is that on August 8, 2023, my husband – pastor – lineman – best friend and father of our three children – was electrocuted after grabbing a powerline that he didn't know had electricity running through it.

The men, those he worked with, the EMS, nurses and doctors, those who worked tirelessly to revive my husband, Brian, soon realized that resuscitating him was not going to happen. This dark moment taught us all that sometimes, there is no hope. While myself and my children, and so many others, hoped Brian would stay here with us, God had bigger plans for Brian. While tears were shed here on earth, the angel's of heaven were singing a welcome song for my husband.

When I walked into the hospital after being told that Brian wasn't going to make it home to me and my three children, I felt my life begin to crumble, my heart begin to tremble and my hope begin to falter. It was during those painful moments that God nudged my spirit and told me why He had taken my husband of 23 years home to be with Him. Once again, I was filled with hope.

With so many prayers prayed by people all over, those who knew Brian best and those who only heard of the event through the papers and radio broadcasts, and the knowledge that God had bigger plans than most could even imagine, I felt my strength reach epic proportions. Although I had just lost the love of my life, I was sure that God had bigger plans, more important motives, a purpose that only He Himself could truly explain. And, quite possibly, I was created for such a time as this!

Even though I am strong because God gives me strength that I can't even explain, I still have had a hard time with this grief. Mourning is something that no one can be prepared for. It is a darkness that hangs onto the spirit the way a tear hangs onto the broken heart. But, HOPE keeps me going. I work to stay on the path God blessed me with, but sometimes I fail. I'm human, despite all my heart's best intentions. While He is always there to pull us out of the filth we find ourselves in, we can get discouraged. But, He always encourages me with that HOPE that leads me toward a home that will never fade away, a hope that will lend my soul the answers that I've yearned for, a hope that comes to the spirit who clings to the Savior for this time on earth.

God has His reasons and He always keeps His promises. I have seen people saved by grace. I have watched them hurt, then grow into something more than they were before they met the Savior. I have come to realize that God always has a plan and even that plan that we don't understand is a plan that will lead to a better outcome than anything our little hearts could have arranged. God's still working on some of us and He is still working on me.

Once, my husband and pastor and best friend, preached that we should pray without ceasing. It takes a heart full of hope to pray that way and today, I'm praying continuously for those who might be losing hope. Listen to that hope that was brought to life by the man named Jesus and hear what He is saying when He saves. He is offering us hope that will never end, hope that is beyond our comprehension.

For whoever reads these words I've written, it is my HOPE that you will reach out to the One who created us all, the One who encourages my heart, the One who has saved my soul. It is Jesus who brings hope to the hopeless and heaven to the undeserving. He is the answer to all those prayers and the reason that I know this hope I have is more than a simple expression of my faith. This is hope that God stirred inside where I believe He will carry out all the plans He has for me and everyone who lives for this Jesus who changed the darkness to light, who changed the wrong and made things right, who comforts the broken and decides to abide inside those who believe He is everything, He is love, for the ones who simply believe.

I hope, when you read this, you find the hope that never leaves.

Colette M. Blankenship

Introduction

Genesis 50:20 "But as for you, ye thought evil against me; but God meant it unto good, to bring to pass, as it is this day, to save much people alive."

I met a woman I'll call Doubt. Doubt resembled me in some ways. She liked to read. She seemed interested in protecting children and animals. But there was something about Doubt that caused me to wonder. Was she a Christian? Did she know the love of God? Was she Jesus' follower? I had to know.

When I first started a conversation about God with Doubt, I was met with an adamant "NO. I do not believe in God! I am an atheist." Atheist! Atheist? Oh, my. I was in for trouble. Despite every reason I had for not following directions when God told me to work His name, His Son's name and Christianity into my conversation with Doubt, I did it. These were unwelcome thoughts I'd placed in the mix for Doubt. Soon, she was letting me know – without any doubt, that my God thoughts were unwelcome.

Hmmm? Could it be that Doubt doth protest too much!? Hmmm?

Finally, I came to realize that I was only stirring the pot, so to speak, with all my meanderings and ramblings about the Lord. Doubt wasn't biting. But, Doubt did love to read. I decided I would offer her one of my books of Christian poetry. As soon as I handed over the volume she retorted, "I won't read it!" "Oh," I told her, "it's poetry." As if she wouldn't have realized that but from my soft reply she seemed to have relaxed a bit. "Ok," she said simply, accepting my token and placing it in a place for later examination.

Just before placing my book in Doubt's hands, I felt the Holy Spirit prompting me to recall that verse that I wasn't apt to think of on my own at all. The verse that says, Matthew 7:6 "Give not that which is holy unto the dogs, neither cast ye your pearls before swine, lest they trample them under their feet, and turn again and rend you." Yes. My books certainly were my small pearls. But, was God telling me to ignore the sinner's heart, the one who needs saving, the one who I felt determined to plant my seed of Him inside? Surely not.

After offering my book to Doubt, and going on about my day, I heard a message that reminded me we have all been those 'swine' at some point in life. Each of us had to hear about Jesus and each of us had to have the opportunity to believe Him. Doubt is no different than me. Yes. Her sin is different than my own, but her need for a Savior is not different at all.

Just after this I was separated from my friend, Doubt. She went her way and I went mine, but I have not one doubt that my ministering to her was well spent. She might not meet my Jesus. She might not get saved. She might go to hell. But, not without my prayers. Not without my sincerely planting the seed that I hope has taken up root in her spirit. Not without the friend who believes, believing that she is indeed one of the souls who has heard the gospel here on earth. She might not take the initiative and become a Christian. But, how am I to know?

I threw my "Pearls" before swine and I believe the One who inspired me to write those words has blessed me all the more, with blessings only my heart can sing of, because – in spite of their dark heart, I ask Him to save the atheist as well as the believer. We are all sinners. We all need a Savior. And, thanks to God, to Jesus, to the blood, we have the freedom – even in our sinful state – to repent, reach out and rest our souls in His embrace. I'm so very thankful that He made a way that only love could have paved. His road is the road to eternal hope, eternal faith, eternal grace. His road is the road to everlasting peace and I am walking this road when I seek to serve the ones that He sought when He came to live, die and rise again. Thanks to Jesus, I am surer than I've ever been that each tear I cry for the lost is a tear that stirs heaven's light so that it reflects what it means for God to silence all fear with His gentle strength.

There is nothing on earth that can change a heart. But when you mention Jesus, you can change the darkest heart. You can change the color of a thought. You can change the fate of what was lost. And, that – my friend, is worth the cost of your service to God.

I hope and I pray, that with these "Pearls" I've written from my heart, there will be one changed so that they'll reach that place where God can take away all their worst and give them a new heart, a new body, a new home in heaven, where He will forever abide with us.

All Doubt aside, let love be the guide! Let love be the guide!

Day One

Jesus loves you

Romans 8:24 For we are saved by hope: but hope that is seen is not hope: for what a man seeth, why doth he yet hope for?

Thanks to Jesus Christ, I have hope that I would never have had if He hadn't come into the world, spent His time—certainly a hard time since He was away from His home, heaven, and His Father, God. He spent His time on earth teaching the disciples to live their lives in service, to give generously, with assurance that they would one day see the king of kings coming back to them on the clouds, glorified and willing to bring them with Him, into the home they had only dreamed of seeing. He lived. He died and He came back in the resurrection. Now, He lives in heaven with His Father, making intercession for those of us who believe, those of us who have the hope that there will come a time when we'll be living there with Him in paradise eternally, forever alive in the timeless light of His love.

Eagerly, we Christians are waiting for that moment when we see Him, face to face, offering His presence as our reward for serving Him, living beneath the power of His grace, His blood, throughout our time on earth. We wait, preparing for that moment—that precious twinkling of an eye when the dead in Christ shall rise. Or, even possibly, rise to the heavens without ever experiencing death here on earth—according to the expected time when He silences the fears that have taunted us and leads the way to eternity with Him.

SO we wait for Him with that cherished treasure, the HOPE that sees us through the darkness into the light of His abundant blessings, into the wonder of His grace and gentle comforting. Thanks to Him, we can know what it means to live with a hope that erases every fear with its faithfulness, destroys the depression and despair with its authenticity, awakens prayers with its truthfulness. Thanks to the HOPE that He stirs to life inside us, we can anticipate His promises, His blessings, His abundant grace. Thanks to the HOPE He whispers through our thoughts, our prayers and praise, our dreams, we can experience a faith that assures us that we have everything we need because we have the One who freed us from the sin that discouraged and disrupted every part of our lives. Thanks to HOPE, we can believe in the future without seeing.

It is in this HOPE He whispers through our spirits that we can truly see, even though we don't see. It is through HOPE that we become certain that His love and grace and return to us is certain. Hope assures us that every struggle, every fear, all the tears are worth it. Soon, much sooner than we think, we'll meet with the One who gave us the HOPE to keep trying, keep believing, keep preparing for that meeting that will bring us into the presence of One far greater than we can imagine seeing. Thanks to HOPE we have the courage to press on toward that eternal home.

A Prayer & A Promise

Dear Lord, I HOPE You know that the very hope that you've inspired inside me is a hope that is so alive it reminds me, each day, to keep trying—to keep smiling—to keep You in the front of mind, where I think of You when any need, any doubt, any fear might silence my Hope. Because You are the most important person in my life, in my soul, I can HOPE beyond hope, beyond any thought or imagining, that You will fill my spirit with eternity when I feel like hesitating on the road to forever with You. Thanks to YOU, Your HOPE—I know what it is to keep listening to Your words when the struggles want to silence my dreams and when the worries want to destroy my peace. Thank You, Lord, for being with me—providing the HOPE I need and reassuring me that, with You, there is enough HOPE to see me through until I meet You in person and worship You eternally. Thank You, Lord, for all You are and all You will one day be. I HOPE You know what You mean to me. I love You with a love that You stirred in me.

> God's mercy and grace give me hope—for myself,
> and for our world.
> —Billy Graham

Day Two

1 Corinthians 9:10 Or saith he it altogether for our sakes? For our sakes, no doubt, this is written: that he that ploweth should plow in hope; and that he that thresheth in hope should be partaker of his hope.

P aul was bringing the gospel to those who needed the gospel desperately—despite the fact that he wasn't always paid for his service, his preaching, his gift of sermons. Sometimes the people he evangelized didn't give him any support, though that was a necessity for him. Though he was in need of their funding, Paul still served and evangelized, bringing the gospel to everyone who might have hoped to hear his word, his sermon, his revelation of the Lord Jesus Christ.

Some hearers, still today, don't believe that we need to provide for the preacher or evangelist. According to the above verse and others in the bible, though, our support (financially and spiritually) is a requirement of the hearer of the good news. We're supposed to give back to the one who gives us the blessing of the gospel preached so that we can hear and understand, so that we can be saved and make it to the promised land. We're meant to give to the preacher even though we don't always do so. He is our minister, our preacher, our pastor—he is our evangelist, our missionary, our vicar. Thanks to him, many find their way into the heaven that is so much better than the hell they were destined for. Thanks to him, it is almost assured they'll spend their entire lives feeling thankful for the gift, the grace, they've been blessed with. And, thanks to him—the preacher—we can realize the importance of our gratitude, our prayer and praise, the appreciation of the One who lived and died and made a way for us to enter paradise.

Thanks to the preacher, there are souls who have discovered the meaning of hope, hope that sustains, hope that abides within the heart and soul, hope that is an open door to grace and faith and love that remains invincible throughout life. Thanks to the preacher, who is often more humble than anyone else in the church, we have the chance to meet with the One who made a way for us. Thanks to the preacher, we can hope without giving up. We can hope for the blessings that withstand all the fears and tears. We can hope for the honor of praying and praising throughout the years. We can hope that He hears everything we say to Him, all the things that we hope brings us into a closer relationship with Him. We hope and that hope is a gift, just like grace and faith. Thanks to Jesus love, our hope will always bring us the answer to despair. With hope, we can make it through the darkness into the light that reflects His beauty, His gentleness, His kindness and sincerity. Thanks to hope, we know what it means to appreciate the preacher who enlightens us and illuminates the wisdoms that prevent us from walking in darkness. Thanks to the hope that our preachers describe so well, we have the opportunity to escape the flames of hell.

A Prayer & A Promise

Dear Lord, You know my heart and You know that, whatever I may be—whether gluttonous or generous, I believe in the words You've brought to me and I've learned so many things from the preachers I've heard along the way. Without them, I would have, so often, been fumbling for the comprehension that helped me to grasp the meaning of Your scriptures. Thanks to the ones You've prepared, the preachers who are so eloquent and sincere, I've learned many things about Your word that I never would have known without their sermons. Thanks to the preachers I've known, I'm more prepared to talk to You and hope that You will talk to me and prepare me to give back to this world a light that You and Your Holy Spirit stir within me. Jesus, help me to always be a blessing to the preachers I meet and to encourage them—both spiritually and financially. Thank You, Jesus, for the hope You bring. I love YOU!

> What gives me the most hope every day is God's grace; knowing that his grace is going to give me the strength for whatever I face, knowing that nothing is a surprise to God.
> —Rick Warren

Day Three

Romans 4:18 Who against hope believed in hope, that he might become the father of many nations, according to that which was spoken, So shall thy seed be.

A braham and Sarah held onto hope even through the darkest valley of impossibility. It seemed like their hope was futile when they thought of their age and the ridiculousness of Sarah birthing a child at such an age. Becoming the father of many nations, as God had told Abraham he would become, seemed hopeless. But, despite the absurdity of hoping for such a thing, Abraham held onto his hope. He believed God and hoped beyond hope that His promises were attainable. He hoped that God was who He said He was and that this God he'd put his faith, his hope, his trust into, would make his dreams a reality one day.

It wouldn't be very long, according to God's timing, before Abraham would become the father he hoped to be and Sarah would hold the baby she'd hoped to embrace. And, even though many years would pass by, it wouldn't be so long before the many nations God spoke of would become a reality that only God Himself could have inspired into reality. Abraham would, indeed, become the father of many nations and those nations would eventually become Israel, God's chosen people.

How many times have I felt like my dreams were hopeless, beyond possibility for me, so incredible that I'd never see them change from being inside my thoughts, my heart . . . to the actuality that showed me God is still at work on behalf of His children. He still stirs dreams to life and He still makes those dreams materialize. He is still bringing my hopes, our hopes, a reason and making them into truth when the perfect moment comes to life. He is still a God of hope, a God of certainty, a God who answers prayers and makes hope something that prepares the way for dreams that will become a reality. Thanks to the Creator who made us we can hope even when it seems like our hope is ridiculous. Through hope, He often fulfills the very dream that seemed doomed to failure.

Hope anticipates the future, the idea, the beautiful. Hope silences the doubt, the dread, the despair. Hope remembers the time when God was faithful, the time when God did—the time when God assured the spirit that hopes truly can be fulfilled. Dreams can come true. His blessings are sure. His light shines even brighter in the darkest moments. Through hope, we will find that light and reach toward more of the wonderful, the amazing, the joyful.. as we praise Him for the hope that He stirs up inside the ones who know His hope is a blessing we're so fortunate to delight in. Hope is alive, a burning smile, a fervent light. Hope is the miracle of a spirit who believes in the One who rouses hope inside even the heart who is desperate, the heart who needs this hope more than anyone, the heart who feels this hope like a gentleness, a healing touch, a blessing sent by the God of love.

A Prayer & A Promise

Dear Lord, I have never been so sure, so hopeful, as I am today—because the more I learn about You and the hope that comes to life inside the soul who believes in Your Son, the more I realize that hoping is second nature to the heart who hears Your tenderness, Your joy, Your sweetness . . . melting away the black dread, the dark depression, the anxieties and doubts. Thanks to the hope You place inside the believer, there is the assurance that whatever comes, You will whisper hope into the heart so that courage and strength become a reality for the one who listens to Your words, Your inspiration, Your support. Thanks to You, dear Lord, I know what it is to feel hope rushing to the rescue when something feels desperate. The more forlorn and fruitless the situation, the more that hope feels like a kindness that only You could have whispered. Yes, Lord, I know that every hope I've ever had hasn't become reality. But, even those hopes that were dashed taught me that, with You beside me, guiding and inspiring me, there is a blessing to be had. It is often in the crushed hope that I've discovered something much more worthwhile than the success that I'd hoped for. Thanks to You, Lord, I know the meaning of success even when my hope is not attained, even when my failure turns to pain, even when I'm drenched by the pouring in rain. Because with You beside me, the rain brings with it the nurturing of hope for a flower that becomes the beautiful from tomorrow's sun, the Son who overcomes every letdown.

> When you say a situation or a person is hopeless,
> you are slamming the door in the face of God.
> —Charles L. Allen

Day Four

Romans 15:13 Now the God of hope fill you with all joy
and peace in believing, that ye may abound in hope,
through the power of the Holy Ghost.

Hope is a living thing. It abides inside those who believe
with a faith that accomplishes so much for the soul. It
is like a summer rain who nurtures and nourishes the
soil, the plants, the pods. It is like the caress of the autumn sun. It
is like the music that is a melody of peacefulness, warmth and love.
Hope is the victory when the end of the day has come and peace
envelops the soul with its powerful smile and erases all the worries
that have traveled with it for the hours of restlessness that taunted
the spirit. Hope is like a moment when light falls down from the
moon, reflecting the beautiful and erasing the dark's sadness.
Hope is the reason that I can honestly say there is the expectation,
the plan, the chance for tomorrow's grace. Hope is inspiration and
faith and everything in between. Hope is the answer when everything else has taken despair as their present impression. Hope is
kindness and affection. Hope is God's direction.

In Romans 15:13, Paul instructs believers to simply 'KEEP
BELIEVING" and abounding in HOPE, because Paul knows that
hope will take the heart so much farther than despair. Hope will
encourage prayer and praise. Hope will produce grace. Hope will
inspire and soothe away the tears. Hope will stir up the happy
heart and melt away the fears. Hope will brighten the spirit and

send peace into the heart who believes in Him. Hope is the way for every believer. Without hope, we are doomed to disbelief and discouragement. Without hope, we're like the world who only hopes for itself, never for the salvation of the human race, salvation that has a chance to take us from this darkness into the heart of a light so alive that is shines into the soul and silences every bleak doubt. With HOPE, we can find our way out of the clouds and into the tenderness of the Son's rays.

Thanks to hope, I know how to cope. Thanks to hope, I know that my soul has a hope and a future. Thanks to hope, I can sincerely believe when, in my mind, I didn't think that was possible for me. Thanks to hope, there is a stirring of grace, the moving of faith, the beauty of His face. Thanks to the hope that He placed in my soul, I can sincerely feel like the impossible is possible, the dreadful—tolerable, the unviable—viable. Thanks to HIM, hope is alive within my spirit and I hope that I can always find a way to reach beyond my own peculiarities into the promises that await me, the promises that He made me when He saved me. Thanks to HOPE, there is a measure of faith, a measure of grace, a measure of thanks—praise for the One who made a way where no way was known before. Thanks to HOPE, the hope He provides—like a child on the inside, I have hope of the improbable, hope of the difficult, hope of the unfeasible. Thanks to hope that He brought, I can reach toward tomorrow believing that the day will dawn beautiful, the heart will smile and the light of His love will shine, reflecting the wonder of a hope that is abundant. My hope for you is that you will keep hoping when it seems hopeless because it is hope that brings hearts through the darkest moments.

A Prayer & A Promise

Dear Lord, I've been hopeless and desperately afraid of the things that fear brought to me. As a child, I was afraid of the dark. As I grew, I feared losing the ones I love. As life passed by me, I feared never doing those things I knew You had for me to do. As time continues on, I fear—yet, I find hope that silences those fears

11

because this hope is a hope that You gave me to delight in. This hope is hopeful of forever, paradise with You, my joy and my Savior. Thanks to You, my dear Lord, there is hope living inside me that silences the worst that comes, erases the worries and fears, reminds me that You are with me through everything. Thanks to You, my Savior, I am not hopeless anymore. I have hope that I never thought possible before. Because of YOU, hope abounds within me and hope restores my believing. Hope is wise and feeds my spirit with a sweetness that only You, in all Your beauty, could have stirred within me. Thank You, Lord, for giving me hope that believes forever is more than possible. Forever is my expectation, my hope of the eternal home You made me. Thank You, Lord, for saving me!

> I place no hope in my strength, nor in my works: but all my confidence is in God my protector, who never abandons those who have put all their hope and thought in him.
> —Francois Rabelais

Day Five

Romans 12:12 Rejoicing in hope; patient in tribulation; continuing instant in prayer;

There is joy in knowing the Lord. There is joy in spite of the heartache. There is true joy even during the dark days. There is joy amid the most severe grief. There is joy that is beyond what our hearts might expect to have because, in life, there are always reasons to despair, to fear, to cry out in sorrow with tears that wash away the beautiful, the hoped for. Although there are so many reasons for suffering and mourning, more losses than I can think of and more to regret than I care to mention—there is still a hope that deserves celebrating. This hope is like a silent ember, smoking with faith and rising just beneath the ashes of grace. Thanks to this hope that is like a miracle to the heart who is feeling so much pain, joy comes to life inside those who believe that He is near, alive in the sparks where His light reflects the endless joy that abides anywhere He is.

Joy falls on the life of the believer like a gentle rain, soothing away all the worst and carrying with it a feeling of tenderness that bleeds compassion into the spirit and mends the ragged edges of indifference. Thanks to the joy that comes with real hope there is comfort that heals the wounds and relieves the frayed and tired anxieties that tremble just beneath the quiet tears. Thanks to this hope that is like a answered prayer, a kiss from heaven, God's embrace for the children He has saved from their sins, there is a peace that feels like light passing across the darkness, whisperings of life beckoning to the spirit to listen, to hear the melody of this hope stirring up joy that is bold and alive. Joy like this comes from abiding in the presence of One far more alive, far more beautiful and wise, far more wonderful than any other I know of. His presence assures and invites the believer into the company of a hope and a joy that can't be imagined by the wildest dreams or the most extreme fantasies. Hope brought to life by Jesus is hope that lasts beyond forever. It is hope that brings with it true freedom and a feeling of joy that astounds and stuns the reasoning.

Thus, even when I feel the darkness falling across my spirt—even when I long for the days when I felt brave and strong—even when I feel like I'm weak beyond what my heart can face . . . even in the worst that comes, I know that the hope He brings to my spirit, the hope that goes to the depths of my feelings, the hope that gives my whole life meaning, is hope that will inspire joy despite whatever I must endure, whatever I must confront and whatever I must bear. Thanks to His gift of hope that lasts through the cruelest griefs, I can experience joy while in the depths of despair. There is a joy that comes with hope, hope of life eternal, that never allows the darkness to erase the promises that He brings when He saves the soul from eternity without His presence. Thanks to this hope and joy, there is assurance that whatever might come God is in control and He knows just what is right for the soul.

A Prayer & A Promise

Dear Lord, You know me and You know what my heart hopes. When your apostle Paul was in prison he hoped and felt joy, even singing and praising. That is what I want to do, Lord—to praise You, even when the hurt stings—to praise You, even when the heart aches—to praise You, even when I don't know what to say. I HOPE, dear Lord, to be filled with the joy of knowing that You're here with me even when I can't feel You. I hope, Lord, that You will hear me praising You amid the darkest moments I face, even when I'm struggling with temptations, even when I lack the words to pray. I hope, dear Lord, that You will understand my prayers and praise, my heart's HOPE, even when I don't understand myself. I hope, dear Lord, that I can be someone who trembles with real joy because I know YOU and the hope you've inspired inside me. Thank You, Lord, for the hope that is so gratifying. Thank You, Lord—for bringing me hope that shines through the worst that comes. I love You, Lord.

> We must accept finite disappointment, but never lose infinite hope.
> —Martin Luther King, Jr.

Day Six

Jesus loves you

Psalms 39:7 And now, Lord, what wait I for?
my hope is in thee.

I t isn't money or material things that makes life worthwhile. It isn't degrees, rewards or scholarly endeavors that bring life the most substantial wealth. It isn't the creation—the sun, the moon, the stars—that brings the most significant source of joy in living. It isn't even the dream that comes true or the idea that brings a truth to life. In spite of what some believe, it is God Himself who brings the ultimate joy, the most beautiful peace, the amazement in living. It is in God that hope comes to life, enlightening, inspiring, inviting the spirit to reach beyond the promise into the reality that comes to life inside those who remember that only God can plant the seed of real love, nourish it with His grace and inspire it to praise with its faith. It is only through God's love that we discover the meaning of praise that even spreads from the depths of doubt and despair. It is this amazing praise that God is looking for when He speaks into the spirit of a hope, a love that is unconditional, thrilling, forever with you.

My hope is in the Lord. My hope is in His promises. My hope is in His victories. My hope is in His sweet grace and peace. My hope is in the love He brings when I listen to Him speak to my spirit. With Him, I know what it is to love without giving in to distrust. With Him, I know what it means to never give up. With Him, I know that this love He provides increases throughout my life, through every fear, through every tear, through every year. Finally, with time, I know what it is to be assured that He is alive and that He lives inside me . . . because I know, without a doubt, that His peace is inviting me to shine a light to the world, a light that never goes out. His light is brighter than any doubt. His light is more beautiful than the sun or moon. His light reflects the miracle of love that sweetens and soothes, love that is everlasting, eternal, forever a part of the wonder that comes to the ones who believe Him and receive Him. He is my hope and my reason. He is incredible. He astonishes the heart who sees Him and invites Him into their heart, where He will stir such a hope that only God Himself could have moved there.

No. It isn't money or things that make life a good place to live. It isn't popularity or intellectual ideas. It isn't the most beautiful sunset or the forest trees. It isn't in the invention or the craftmanship. It isn't in the artistic or poetic that beautiful stills with its breathlessness. It isn't in any of the blessings He gives that we find our true hope. It is only in the living God, the One who created us all, the One who lives to bring us blessings and HOPE, that we feel inspired to HOPE with a HOPE that is eternal, a HOPE that is a living thing, a HOPE that frees us to hear Him. Thanks to the hope that he brings there is a wonder that comes to life inside those who remember to shout out praise for the God we believe, the One we need when nothing seems to work for us, the One who brings a hope and a peace that is more powerful than any force on earth. Thanks to the God of the universe, the God who is light, the God who is love . . . I know hope that has awakened joy and love inside my spirit. Thanks to the Hope He brings with Him, I will never need to feel desperate or doomed. I can always know a hope that assures my heart that God is in control of it all and God won't let me despair for too long. Thanks to Him, hope brings me the courage to go on.

A Prayer & A Promise

Dear Lord, You said that David was a man after Your heart. David's words, His psalms, stir up the light in the heart who hears his writings, his words of praise, his spiritual prayers. I, too, love David and his writings. And, I too, hope that—when You hear my praise—You will smile with gladness because Your child, the one who aspires to bring the world a bit of Your light with her poetry and prose, the one who HOPES to bring You a bit of the praise that is living inside her, where she knows that YOU abide with her—because she has pleased You. Lord, I want to please You. I want to be the woman You know as friend, the woman You know as kind, the woman You know as the believer who brings You the greatest admiration, the worship and praise that silences the darkness. I hope that You will see in me, dear Lord, the peace and the joy that You gave me when You saved me. Thank You, Lord, for freeing me from the past sin, for bringing me to a place of victory where I win the greatest blessing of all, the blessing of a hope that comes to life in those who know that You are the hope of the world. You are the hope that assures and comforts. You are the hope that promises love that lives forever, where we'll always be together.

> Hope is like the sun, which, as we journey toward it, casts the shadow of our burden behind us.
> —Samuel Smiles

Day Seven

Psalms 119:114 Thou art my hiding place and my shield:
I hope in thy word.

There is so much hope in God's word. There is hope for joy and peace. There is hope for His saving grace. There is hope for the life being lived and there is hope for the life that will soon be. Hope is found in His word when it convicts and when it inspires and when it brings a promise. It is found in His word when it brings concern and when it silences the darkest fear. It is found in His word when it reminds us to give and when it gives to us a peace that is beyond our comprehension. It is found in His word when it encourages and when it stirs up burning desire. Hope is found in God's words when it reminds us to pray and when it prompts our praise. Hope is found in God's word, in so many verses and chapters, in those scriptures that reveal His love and in those scriptures that expose His light. Hope is found through, not only the psalmist who wrote the verse above, but also through John when He penned revelation and reassured our hearts that Jesus would, indeed, come again to bring His church back to the promised home where He lives, making intercession for you and me.

He surely is a God of hope. Without Him, without His love, I would likely be on the verge of suicide. Without Him, His grace and love, I wouldn't know what it means to give without thinking of myself first. Without Him and the hope He brought to each one of us when He came into this world and died on a cross and rose again to defeat death, hell and the grave . . . none of us would have the hope that He stirred up in everyone when He rose into the clouds on His way to heaven and the Father's presence. Without Jesus and the hope He brings with Him when He takes up residence inside a soul, there would be no victory in living. Without Him, hope would be futile. There would be no dream, no vision, no satisfaction. Without Him and the hope He inspires within the soul, there would be no salvation to take away the sins that reveal the messiness of our souls. Without Him and the hope He brings with Him when He silences sin with His gift of grace, there would be no reason to go through this dark world and bring light to a human race who thinks it has no need of His grace.

He is my hiding place and my shield. He is my hope and my reason for living and giving. He is my everything and I can't possibly imagine a hope that isn't inspired by the miracle of His sacrifice, His gift of grace, His assurance and love. Thanks to the God of love, the God who is love, the God who actually gave us His only Son, there is hope for eternity with Him, the only One who really makes a difference inside the heart who is convicted. Thanks to Him and His love, this hope that stirs up kindness and light, brightens the fires of joy and insight, breathes praise and prayer throughout my time here—I know that Jesus will be with me, restoring and inspiring, making me into the child of God who He died for. It is my greatest hope, that someday, someway, I can be the child He aspires to make me.

A Prayer & A Promise

Dear Lord, Thanks to You and all You've done for me, I can enter into eternal life when my time on earth is through. Thanks to You, I have a hope that is beyond wonderful. It is a hope that is alive and echoes with praises for You, the One who created me and the One who changed me, the One who makes a way for me even when I can't see past that closed door in my way. Thank You, Jesus, for loving me through all that dark in my life and bringing me out of the shadows, into the grace, the flow of love, the light that comes from knowing You and the miracle of Your love. Thank You, Jesus, for giving me a hope and a future. Thank You for guiding me out of sin and into the life that I would never have dreamed I'd have. Thanks to You, the hope You brought to me, I know what it means to love unselfishly, with a love that You stirred up within when I became a woman who knows You as my best friend. Thank YOU, Lord. You're the greatest love I've ever known or hoped to know.

What gives me the most hope every day is God's grace; knowing that his grace is going to give me the strength for whatever I face, knowing that nothing is a surprise to God.
—Rick Warren

Day Eight

2 Corinthians 3:12 Seeing then that we have such hope,
we use great plainness of speech.

As an associate at Walmart I came across such a variety of human natures and personalities. I met with kindness and I met with meanness. I met with inspiring and I met with apathetic. I met with understanding and I met with insensitive. I met with believers and I met with those who don't believe in God.

During one particular meeting, I was introduced to a woman who was an atheist. She so strongly BELIEVED in not believing that she wouldn't even consider the possibility of a redeemer. She turned my every opportunity to nudge her into belief into a strong dispute, so I didn't attempt to quarrel with her. I did ask her, quite strongly, where—if she didn't trust in Jesus—did she find HOPE?! And, I did pray for her, for her soul, for her salvation from the darkness that she was living in. As I became reluctant to discuss faith with this woman with hopes of persuading her into Christianity, a few months into meeting her, I decided to give her one of my books of Christian poetry in the chance that this would influence her and guide her toward the truth of Jesus.

As I was on my way to work that morning, with the book—Gift of Grace—lying in the seat next to me, a specific verse that I wasn't usually called to kept floating into my thoughts. (Matthew 7:6 (KJV) "Give not that which is holy unto the dogs, neither cast ye your pearls before swine, lest they trample them under their feet, and turn again and rend you."). It took a bit of thought before I realized that, yes, oh yes . . . I was throwing my pearls before swine. Despite hearing that specific verse over and over in my thoughts, I decided to offer the woman my book, my "pearl" with the hopes that it would touch her heart and direct her toward the One (the greatest PEARL of all pearls) who could make a way for her to find the saving grace, the HOPE that I rely on so completely.

When I offered this woman, who admitted to being an avid reader, my book—she said "I won't read it" and I told her mildly, "it's poetry." Finally, she accepted my "gift." A few days later, dispelling every reluctant thought I might have had, I heard a sermon on that very verse about pearls and swine which told me that we have all been the swine at some point because we have all, needless to say, been sinners in need of saving. This woman accepted my Gift of Grace and we never spoke of the gift again. She quit her job at Walmart soon after that and I didn't hear from her again but I still pray that she finds her way into the Christian faith and a relationship with the One who makes a way out of the darkness that I know she is living in when she admits that she is, indeed, an atheist who tries to discourage other Christians from their faith. As I write this entry into the devotional, Pearls of Hope, I HOPE that each of my readers will take this opportunity to pray for, not only this woman I met on my journey, but all the nonbelievers who need saving from the darkness, the doubting, the despair—death without a Savior, death that will bring them to a destiny of fire and brimstone, a hell that is beyond hopeless, a hell that is complete doom for the soul, throughout eternity.

A Prayer & A Promise

Dear Lord, I'm praying today for every nonbeliever, for their souls to find You, the whole reason for life and love, the whole joy in believing in Your grace, the whole wonder of being saved from this hell that comes to those who refuse Your kindness, Your saving grace, Your hope for eternity with God. Please, Lord, save the lost souls that wander around this life without a hope, without faith, without the joy of seeing YOU are the way. Please, Lord, seek that which is lost and save them from the darkness. Give each of us the opportunity to bring Your light into the darkest parts of the world, to reflect Your beauty, Your grace, Your peace. Give each one of Your children a chance to tell the world about You. Whether it is through our lifestyles, our writings or words, our gifts or giving, our kindness, our hearts or whether it is through the miracle of grace that is Your greatest blessing—I pray, dear Lord, that You will give us the chance to give someone else the grace and the message that reveals the faith that inspires souls to be saved. Thank You, Lord, for the HOPE that You gave us and the HOPE that saves. Thank YOU, Jesus, for everything!

Hope will never be silent.
—Harvey Milk

Day Nine

Psalms 16:9 Therefore my heart is glad, and my glory rejoiceth: my flesh also shall rest in hope.

David, a man after God's own heart, praised and praised and praised some more. He knew God would bless him even though he wasn't perfect. He was just a man but he was a man who truly loved God and who truly worshipped (in spirit). He gave, not just a part of himself, but his entire heart to the One who created him and gave him all the blessings that would make his life seem like a dream come true. He became a king that would forever be remembered and who would forever inspire others with his praise, his psalms, who brought believers just the right words to encourage their own praise and worship. David's psalms were like tender kisses against God's cheek. He gave parts of his heart, with his inspirations, that most can only dream of bestowing on the Creator, the One who gave each one of us grace and love beyond what we might have hoped or dreamed of. Thanks to David, we have the psalms to guide our worship and his sincerity to show us just what it means to believe and devote our spirits to the One who is the giver of life, the giver of hope, the giver of love that is beyond words. Thanks to David, we know what it means to truly praise.

Yes! My heart, too, is glad and I am always rejoicing and resting in the hope of heaven, of forever, of eternity with the One who made me and saved me. Thanks to this hope I never feel like

I'm doomed to a life and eternity without the joy of living with a Savior who makes a way for me. Thanks to this hope, I am certain that God loves me. Afterall, He sent His SON for me. He gave me the best of the best and taught me, throughout my life, that this love He offered is a love that is more alive, more beautiful and more praiseworthy than anything I could possibly imagine or think of. His love and the hope of eternity with Him, the One who is LOVE, assures my spirit that I never have to worry or fear. I never have to doubt or despair. I never need to think of anything as impossible because with Him, all things are possible. He is the maker of the world, the heart, the hope that restores and reflects this love that is His gift to every believer. Thanks to HIM, this HOPE is a HOPE beyond reason, a HOPE beyond envisioning, a HOPE beyond conceiving. This HOPE He brings to the believer is like a light that never goes out. It silences every doubt and it reflects all the wonder of being guided by the ONE who shares His love, His hope, His peace—grace that is the answer to every heart's desire. He is wise and His wisdom prepares the spirit to feel a fire that can only be found in the burning love poured out inside the hearts who believe in Him.

Like David, I praise Him. Like David, I thank Him. Like David, I HOPE in HIM, the God I know is my very best friend, the God I know is the whisper in the wind, the breathless in the prayer, the maker of darkness and light. Light that glistens just beyond the night. He encourages and reassures. He inspires and sends His sweet love. He is the hope for more than the world. He is the hope that means one day, someday, I will praise Him face to face. I will know the meaning of all those things that I keep believing even when I can't see them. Thanks to HIM, I have a reason to hope when others turn away from His grace without discovering the joy that abides in the presence of the One who makes a way through all the pain, through the rain even though He has nothing to gain—except me, a woman who is so unworthy of the love He offers. He is the hope that leaves me without a doubt—He is the way through every cloud. He is my hope when I can't find a way out. Thanks to God, I have hope of eternity in heaven where I'll live with HIM forever.

A Prayer & A Promise

Thank You, Lord, for bringing me through every discouragement and heartbreak. Thank You for destroying the fears and wiping away the tears. Thank You for reassuring me when I wasn't sure what road to take. Thank You for finding me in the middle of my doubt and silencing the worries and despair. Thank You for bringing me through the darkness, lighting up the dawn of my life with a kindness, a hope that stirs up joy beyond my wildest dreams. Because of YOU, Lord, I know what it means to hope with a hope that is so real, a hope that fulfills, a hope that can inspire me to survive the worst of times with my dreams intact, never looking back . . . because, with YOU, Lord—I have found the answer to my every need. You are the HOPE that I seek. You bring me true peace. Thank You, Lord.

> Hope is the word which God has written on the brow
> of every man.
> —Victor Hugo

Day Ten

1 Corinthians 15:19 If in this life only we have hope in Christ, we are of all men most miserable.

This is where I fall silent . . . many in this world don't believe Jesus rose from the dead. They believe He was a great man, a great teacher and even a great preacher. But, they refuse to believe in His resurrection. This unbelief in the truth of the resurrection is the most pitiful of any doubt I could imagine. It is, just like Paul says in the above verse, the believer who is the most pathetic if there was no resurrection.

But, there was a resurrection. Jesus lived, died and was buried. Then, He rose again on the third day, showing the world that He had given them the opportunity to experience eternal life with Him in heaven. Thanks to this truth, Christians aren't pathetic, but commendable. Their belief is one that brings the lowest of the low to faith, while bringing the greatest of the great to the faith at the same time. It is a belief that doesn't practice any bias or partiality. It allows any and all who believe to share in the faith that brings each of us the grace and the victory. Together, we are the church of Jesus Christ and we'll someday venture, all together, into paradise.

Heaven is our greatest HOPE. It is the hope we have in Christ and the hope that abides inside every heart who knows Him as life that brings us through the darkest lows and still abides with us when we're riding high in the bluest of skies. Thanks to this faith that reminds me everyday, I'm saved to the uttermost, I carry a hope that brings me through life with the feeling that I've been gifted the greatest gift I could have ever hoped for. Indeed, my salvation is the greatest gift I might have hoped for. It is a gift brought to me through grace because I couldn't have earned it. Working for this gift is useless and ineffective. It comes to the believer who has been given grace from God, our Creator and our only HOPE for a future in heaven. Thanks to Him, His grace and love, the hope that abides is a hope that reminds me I'm only alive because He survived. He rose again to shine His light into every soul who believes HE IS the only sacrifice we'll ever need for the sins that we might have thought unforgivable, the same sins that, because of Him, have been forgiven.

Thanks to Jesus' resurrection, I can sincerely pray for the peace that passeth all understanding, the sweetness of forever, the kindness and acceptance that bring me out of the darkness and into the presence of the One who shed His blood, died and rose again so that I can know the meaning of hope, the meaning of grace, the meaning of faith and the meaning of love that is more beautiful than anything on earth. Thanks to Him and His rising again . . . I know what it means to hope when everywhere I look there is hopelessness. Thanks to Him, I hope for more than this world could ever give. I hope for the miracle of life eternal with the One I know as the Savior and my everything.

A Prayer & A Promise

Dear Lord, You're a Savior who knows me so well that You can always tell when I am afraid, when I'm doubting, when I'm in need of Your grace and the hope that makes a way for me to keep trying when I might feel like giving up. Thanks to You knowing me so well, You showed me the way out of my own personal hell AND the way out of the hell that comes to the one who dies without believing in You. Thanks to YOU, Jesus, I know the meaning of a love that has freed me, a love that prepares me, a love that restores and answers me when I need a friend to silence my doubts and place faith inside my heart. Thanks to You, Lord, I know the meaning of conviction and the meaning of forgiveness. Because I know You and have the hope of forever in heaven. I am more joyful, more grateful, more empathetic and sympathetic, more able to shine the light You gave me. Thanks to You, Jesus—I have a hope that survives the darkest nights. Thanks to You, I have a hope that makes me capable of leaving this world without fear of the next life. Thank You, Lord, for the hope that assures me You're with me and one day, You'll greet me in paradise!

I place no hope in my strength, nor in my works: but all my confidence is in God my protector, who never abandons those who have put all their hope and thought in him.
—Francois Rabelais

Day Eleven

Jesus loves you

Psalms 31:24 Be of good courage, and he shall strengthen your heart, all ye that hope in the LORD.

When darkness falls all around my spirit and I can't find my way through the sorrows, the challenges, the disillusionments . . . there is a place where I know that I can find hope for this worry, courage for this trial, confidence for this struggle. When I'm uncertain and the burdens seem like liquid doubt raining down dread and filling my head with fears, my heart with tears, I reach out to the One who silences the wind, quiets the storm, erases the sins that seek to destroy my hope. I reach out to the One who makes a way where no way has been, the One who feeds my spirit with His truth, the One who colors the stars in glistening reflections of kindness and grace. Thanks to the One who feeds my soul with hope, I can always find the light illuminating my shadows and revealing the magnificent that revivifies my worst clouds.

Thanks to the Son, I don't have to worry about anything or anyone. He is the hope that takes away every dread, every doubt, every desperation. The hope He stirs up in the spirit is a hope for the moment when I'll meet Him face to face and experience the pure bliss, the clear beauty, the most genuine peace that I could ever imagine knowing. Thanks to Him, I know the meaning of a love that goes beyond tender. His love convicts and convinces. His love proves and provides. His love is stronger than any feeling. It is the meaning beneath joy, the wonder in wonderful, the music in the heart's hope. Thanks to this amazing person, Jesus, Lord and Savior, I know what it is to hope for everlasting life, eternity in heaven, forever praising the One who lived and died so that you and I could enter into the relationship that is more beautiful than any union the heart could ever think of.

I have a hope that is everlasting, a hope that is eternal, a hope that silences all worry. The breathless whisper of grace that was poured out on the world by the light who guides every heart to the Father, is a grace that reminds the heart of its guilt yet never condemns the spirit. It sends forgiveness that is a true miracle, forgiveness that is unbelievable and, yet, I believe. I believe in His gift with a hope that only comes to life for those who have been to the foot of the cross and learned that there, at His cross, there is a key that unlocks the prison doors of a sin jail where the spirit has been captive, caged by guilt and shame, confined to the weight of sin that penetrates every good thing with its darkness, its doubt, its cloud of immorality.

Through God's one and only Son, there comes a hope that is beyond words, beyond dreams, beyond believing.. Yet, I believe! I believe that He has saved me because I felt the weight of my sin fall away and I felt the load I was carrying become light as a feather, light in a way that is amazing, light so beautiful and startling that it brings the heart a hope that can never be silenced, a hope that abides in the worst situations, a hope that reassures. There is confidence in the One who made a way for anyone who simply believes, has faith, that He is the One who came to save the world. He is the One, the Son, Jesus—Lord of Lords, who made a way for the soul to know Him and be with Him eternally. Thank God for His saving grace, the light who erases the past sin and reassures the believer that, with Him, there is real freedom.

A Prayer & A Promise

Dear Lord, I can never thank You enough for saving me and making me into the woman that I am today—the woman that I will be when You have changed me completely, changed me into the woman I believe You want me to be. I will never be able to thank You enough for all You've done for me. You've brought me through the dark into the light where I can see YOU, the answer to my fight. You challenge me and give me the strength, the inspiration, the grace to meet every challenge with the assurance that, with You, all things are possible. You are my hope. You are the hope that brings me through the very worst there is, silencing my doubts and fears, wiping out all the feelings of dread. You are my hope, the hope that knows—together, with the love You've given me—there is a forever that will bring my soul the victory. Thank You, Lord, for saving me!

> Hope is the only bee that makes honey without flowers.
> —Robert Green Ingersoll

Day Twelve

Psalms 119:116 Uphold me according unto thy word, that I may live: and let me not be ashamed of my hope.

Being different feels wrong somehow when you're a little girl trying to make friends with other children. Having curly hair when most of the other girls have straight hair feels like a nuisance that will jeopardize your possibilities of making friends. A gap between two front teeth can be one of the most annoying features when it seems that most of the other children have teeth that are straight and nested together in their smiles. A hillbilly background that remembers things most of the other children never speak of—things like milking a cow, slopping a hog, hoeing a garden or stacking wood in the woodshed are all reasons to bring the childish heart a wince of fear that she would never be accepted by the other children she met. With a Granny who worried about her children and a Pa who plowed the fields with his workhorse, I felt unlike most of the children I met during my encounters in the school yard.

I didn't think the other children were different at all. I thought it was me that was unusual and odd. I felt like the curiosity, the peculiarity, the quirk in the system that led me to believe I was wrong for being different. Even though I never felt the least reproach when I was met with other's differences, I felt ashamed because of my differences. Afterall, I thought to myself, I had to be wrong. And, yes, even my faith felt like a dissimilarity that I should be ashamed of. I never heard anyone else mention Jesus, the One I'd been encouraged to believe in. I'm not sure when I reached the age of accountability, but before that time, during my early days in school, I felt like the oddball when I remembered this Jesus who everyone at church sung hymns of, preached on and praised. Despite my early teaching about Jesus, I was quiet about my faith and about the many ways that my family and myself were different (or so I thought) than the other children and their families.

It would be years before I put my hope in Jesus with faith that reminded me that being different isn't such a bad thing after all. Being different means set apart, both in ideas and minds. Being different means that when I read a book instead of playing some sport, I was being the girl who would one day want to write a book. Being different meant that my heart melted when I prayed to the One who created me and gave me the nudge in my spirit to put my faith and hope in this Savior, this love who convinced me that He could and would save me to the uttermost. Thanks to my differences I would learn things that others I met along my journey through life would never experience or realize. Thanks to the hope that He stirred inside, my life would sometimes be a roller coaster ride of lessons but, through it all, I'd know that He knew just how much fear I could handle. Thanks to the hope that He whispered into my heart, I know what it means to hear His voice in the silence of dawn, in the blessings He chooses to pour out in my life, in the music that comes from joy He places in my smile.

Because I grew and finally knew that different is, sometimes, a beautiful only God could bless the soul with, I haven't felt that old shame in a very long time. Thanks to the hope He gave me, I know that my differences make me the clay He can mold, the compassion He can grow, the light that is bold. Thanks to the hope He gave me and you, we can glory in our differences and find the courage to face each exception to the norm with assurance that whoever we are, there is One who knows us better than we know ourselves. There is One who loves us better than even the best parents. Thanks to Him I have hope for eternity in His presence where my differences are my best blessings.

A Prayer & A Promise

Dear Lord, because of You, I have a hope that never runs out. This hope is the reminder that love is alive and it is the light that You sparked inside my spirit. Thanks to the hope You gave me when You saved me, I know a joy and a peace that is beyond just different. It is unlike any amazing that can be remembered. Thanks to the hope You gave me, I am more alive than I have ever been before. Because of this hope, even though I've been through more heartaches than I ever imagined possible, I've come out of the darkest valleys with this great hope You gave surrounding me and preparing me, abiding inside where I am certain You have taken up residence, giving me the miracle of Your Holy Spirit, Your gift, Your comfort, You blessing. Thank You, Lord—You are amazing beyond any words!

> Forgiving does not erase the bitter past. A healed memory is not a deleted memory. Instead, forgiving what we cannot forget creates a new way to remember. We change the memory of our past into a hope for our future.
> —Lewis B. Smedes

Day Thirteen

Acts 2:26 Therefore did my heart rejoice, and my tongue was glad; moreover also my flesh shall rest in hope.

Resting in hope is a basic principle of Christianity. We all rest in hope when we come to Jesus, our Lord and Savior. We realize that all hope lies in Him, the Author and Finisher of our faith. He is the way, the truth and the life. He is the answer to every need, the reason for every beautiful thing, the wonder that blesses our hearts and souls with joy. Because we've experienced a relationship with the One who created us and gave us the opportunity to discover the inspiration that is only alive because He lived and died and was resurrected—then, moved to paradise in heaven . . . because we have experienced the King of Kings, the peace that flows down from His spirit, His Holy Spirit, we can be sure that this hope we have only grows larger and more alive with the passage of time.

In this verse, Peter is citing King David (Psalm 16:8–11) to establish that Jesus of Nazareth is the Messiah. He is the hope that sustains us. He reminds us that, like David, we have a hope that is beyond wise. It is wisdom personified. It is light. It is life. It is the reason that we can smile in the midst of troubled times. It is the hope that rises to the forefront when we're at the center of the storm. This hope is like a gift from the heart of the One who created us, blessed us and protects us. Thanks to Him, we know the meaning of hope that is everlasting, hope that is alive, hope that abides inside the heart who knows the meaning of life, the meaning of His sacrifice. Thanks to the hope that comes to life because Jesus gave us His life, I know that I can someday enter the gates of heaven and come to the Father of all life with the hope that He will accept me. Because Jesus lived and died and rose again, I have a hope that is beyond my own comprehension, but it is a hope that satisfies every fear, convinces every doubt, restores every heart.

My heart, like Peter said, does rejoice. The more I seek Him, the more I find Him. The more I believe Him, the more I hope in Him. The more I live for Him, the more I find myself agreeing with His words, His deeds, His invitation to follow Him through life and into eternity where I can forever know the meaning He brings to those who listen, who hear His still, small voice in everything. Because of Him, I rejoice, praise, pray. I know that, because He lives, I have everything I'll ever need. I have the light that pierces through my pain, my worry, my fear . . . light that shines into the darkest dread destroying the darkness. Because of Him, His light, I can see my way through everything that comes, even those moments that are haunted by doubt and doom. Even amid the worst struggles, I have a Savior who reassures me and makes me see that I still can rejoice because, once and for all, He claims the victory. He will always be my choice.

A Prayer & A Promise

Dear Lord, I choose YOU. You are the hope that brings me through the sorrows, the struggles, the situations that make me cringe and fill me with fear, anxiety and worry. Because of You, the hope You stir up inside me, I never need to wallow in the painfulness of doubt. Because I know You, the maker of peace, I can feel a peace that surpasseth all understanding. Because of the hope You've given me, I never have to feel like I am despairing of a way through the darkness. I have a light that guides me past the worst life brings, a light that shines brighter than any light I've ever seen, a light that reminds me there is hope more worthy than any hope that I might dream of. Because of the hope I have in You, precious

Savior, I am more grateful and filled with more joy than I could have ever imagined. Thanks to You, Lord, I know what it is to delight in You and know the beauty of believing in eternity with the One who makes a way for me. Thanks to You, Lord, I am saved to the uttermost. Thank You, Lord. I love You.

> We must accept finite disappointment, but never lose infinite hope.
> —Martin Luther King, Jr.

Day Fourteen

Romans 5:2 By whom also we have access by faith into this grace wherein we stand, and rejoice in hope of the glory of God.

Rejoicing doesn't always come naturally to people. There is so much in this life to bring the heart pain and sorrow, to tempt the thoughts to remember the darkness, to color the dreams in hues of melancholy. Through the life we're living on earth, there are struggles and troubles, worries and fears, regrets and tears that burden our hearts, our souls, our minds. They trouble many of us all the time so that we may have a difficult time 'rejoicing' despite our hope for the everlasting life that God has promised believers in His Son. Even though we have more than enough reason to rejoice when we remember what God has done for us, we still don't always have it in us to rejoice with a heart full of hope and joy.

No, we don't always feel like rejoicing, but nonetheless, we still have plenty of reason in our hearts and souls, reasons like salvation—hope that never fears, hope that is forever, promising to lead us through the years, hope that remembers to wipe away our lonely tears—because of all that God has blessed our souls with we have so much to be thankful for, so much to praise Him for, so much to rejoice over. Even in our darkest moments, if we can simply remember the truth that abides inside, the truth of forever with the One who died but returned to bring us a new life, we can rejoice through the worst that comes. Despite all the sorrows and fears, the worries and tears, we have so very much to rejoice over.

Rejoicing may be a challenge at times but it is something the heart needs to do in order to give God the praise that He so truly deserves. If I think about it, and remember, I deserved God's judgement instead of His grace . . . I deserved the darkness instead of the light, the condemnation instead of the absolution He gave me—then, I remember that I have more to rejoice over than I could ever even think of. My mind won't wrap around the amazing that is His grace, the beauty that He awakens, the wonder that comes from knowing He is there with me, just a prayer away.

Thanks to God, I have a hope that never lets me down. When I feel the worst I've ever felt, I can still go to Him, the joy of my soul, the wonder of my world, the light that lifts me up. Because I know Him as Savior I never have to worry about being enough or believing enough or bringing Him enough of my love. Because HE IS LOVE, I have a hope that is beyond any dream or ambition. This hope for everlasting life is real and true. It means that I have forever with the One who created me and saved me, to look forward to. I have a hope that is more than a desire. It is the blazing fire that lives inside me, always rejoicing because I know that, with Him, I have the answer to my every prayer. Because of Him, this hope that lives inside me gives me a reason to always believe Him. He is always faithful.

A Prayer & A Promise

Dear Lord, even when I'm not faithful, when I doubt, when I worry and when I let the clouds of the darkest dread form in my head, You are still faithful. You are still there, making a way through the fears, erasing all the tears and promising that, throughout the years, You will be there for me, a guiding light, a reflection of the love that only God could have promised me. Thanks to You, sweet Jesus, I know the meaning of a second chance, the promise of unending peace, the joy that takes away all doubt. Because of You, my Savior, I know what it is to hope without doubting, to believe in the everlasting, the know that You are faithful and I never need to dread the future again . . . because You are there, my future—alive and waiting for the moment when I need Your light to shine through the shadows that haunt me and reflect the joy of knowing You are alive and because of You, I will survive whatever comes. You are the hope that I know will never leave me lost. You saved me despite what it cost You. Thank You, Lord. I love You.

God's mercy and grace give me hope
—for myself, and for our world.
—Billy Graham

Day Fifteen

Psalms 130:5 I wait for the LORD, my soul doth wait,
and in his word do I hope.

I can be so impatient. It isn't always easy for me to wait. When I'm waiting, I sometimes fidget with this or that until the waiting seems even more unbearable than if I'd merely taken up a book, His book, and possibly discovered the purpose of my waiting, the hope in His word that would enlighten me and fill me with the wisdom that, quite probably, I'd been waiting for.

He is a good, good God and I don't believe He has ever been angry with me because of my fidgeting when waiting—doing things like playing with my phone, toggling through the Facebook or Twitter world, searching some shopping site that is undoubtedly out of my price range and too expensive to consider. Sometimes I have fidgeted at home, working quickly at venturing from the kitchen to the dining area, never lifting a finger to the work that would have helped my home to look a little more presentable— but, simply pacing and watching the progress of some plant or tree growing, some bird's consuming its dinner, some bee sampling each blossom. Fidgeting can also mean that I squirm and twitch, wriggling through the impossible waiting, never allowing His peace to penetrate my spiritual fretting. It is in the fidgeting that I often discover I'm not as sensible as I would like to think I am. Afterall, I'm acting like a squirming two year old who hasn't found out they don't need the sucker before leaving the store.

God is so so good, though. He never lets me wait without reminding me that it has often been in that very waiting period when I've found the answer. Amid all that squirming and fretting, I've discovered the prayer, the praise, the promise that makes a way through the tears, through the fears, through the years of struggling with whatever I might be waiting for God to erase from my life or place in my life. And, while I wait, if I take just a bit of time for His word (as is mentioned in the above verse), I learn, I grow, I discover and I become someone more because I've taken time in the word of God.

Through His scriptures, I have found the meanings, the requirements, the cause, the significance. Through His word, I've found the answers so many more times than I could count. In His word, I've found—not just answers—but resolutions, grace, blessings that reflect His kindness and beauty, His gentleness and reassurance, His comfort and peace. Through the intimacy of His scriptures I've discovered the love that is God, the love that gives the heart hope, the love that reminds me, through Him, I can know the meaning of life without end. Thanks to Him, this hope for everlasting peace and love is a hope that promises to bring me through the time of waiting into the satisfaction of His grace.

My hope is in Him and I'm certain that, through His word, I will find that waiting can be more than a time for fidgeting or worrying. It can be a time for reflecting and praying. It can be a time for hope that makes a way through every doubt, protects and heals, inspires the soul to trust in His wisdom. Thanks to the hope He gives me, I know what it is to feel peaceful and still as I wait.

A Prayer & A Promise

Dear Lord, You know my heart and You know the parts of me that try to get out of the waiting room, the parts of me that fidget when I should be praying, the parts of me that can't seem to understand Your word will embrace me when I feel the least embraceable. You know how fidgety I can be, but thanks to Your grace and the hope that You bring, I never need to feel like this waiting is beyond my understanding, my acceptance, my lesson. Thanks to You, there is always a teachable moment in the waiting (as there is with everything) and You usually show me something worthwhile through every mile I walk. Thanks to You, there are lessons in the waiting, lessons in the word, lessons in the prayers. Thanks to You, even though I'm not always a quick learner, I do learn and grow and thanks to You, I have become more certain that this hope I have in You, dear Lord, is a hope that will see me through this life into the next where I can meet You face to face. Thank You, Lord. I love You more than I can say.

All human wisdom is summed up in two words; wait and hope.
—Alexandre Dumas

Day Sixteen

Jesus loves you

Job 7:6 My days are swifter than a weaver's shuttle, and are spent without hope.

There are hard times in life. Hard times can come when someone's health leaves them vulnerable and afraid. Hard times come when someone loses everything they've earned with their sweat, blood and tears—and they're financially destroyed. Hard times come in lost homes, lost marriages, lost children, lost hearts. Hard times come when the soul is filled with sorrow and pain, when the spirit is desolate and there is nothing but rain. Hard times come to those who believe and those who don't believe. The difference in the two polar opposites is that the believer has someone, a very big someone, to turn to when the hard times feel like they can't be overcome. Thanks to a loving God who doesn't leave us without any chance of redemption, there is HOPE—even when we experience times, like Job did, when there is only hopelessness to accompany us from point A to point B and it doesn't feel like there is a possibility of joy to come into this sorrow that surrounds us.

Job was, undoubtedly, hopeless. He lost more than most anyone and was drowning in a hopeless that is beyond my own understanding. His hopeless was like misery to the utmost, impossible to the greatest extent of the word, despairing beyond what words might explain. His hopeless wasn't measured in mere degrees. His hopeless was measured in an intensity beyond what darkness or bitterness or regret might portray. His hopeless was more than a fading feeling, depression or darkness. His hopeless braved the waters of a melancholy, a fearfulness, a agony that I can only speak of. I can't understand it. I can't empathize with him. I can only sympathize to the point of knowing he was hurting in ways that can't be exposed. His hurt was like flames scorching away every hope in the soul. If I ever find myself on the brink of despair I remember Job and reconsider my own situation. Where I might feel I'm lacking or in need—where I might feel like I'm bleeding the blood of despair, I remember this fellow, Job, who bled the entire meaning of hopeless in ways that I will not think of.

I can't remember Job without thinking of the hopelessness he must have endured. Job loved God more than I could imagine. Could I even think of being as true to the One who brought me out of my own darkness into the light of a love that is brimming with goodness and joy? I have my doubts that I could possibly be as brave and brilliant, as wise and wonderful, as authentic and genuine as this man that God trusted so much that He actually allowed the devil to test him with so many trials that most would have died in the flames of the ordeal. Job was someone who upheld His faith in God and gave the world a reason to hear his message of hope that wins when everything predicts futility.

Yes, of course Job felt hopeless. But, he didn't fail the test. He overcame because he placed his faith in the One who makes a way when there seems to be no road but the hard road. Sometimes, when all we see is pain up ahead, there rises up a reason, a blessing, a hope that we would never have imagined. Thanks to the One who created us and continues to abide with us, blessing us, there is always hope waiting just beyond the next curve. Thanks to God and His amazing gift of grace . . . the Son who makes a way

. . . there is hope that is more alive than anything else I can think of. Thanks to God, there is a hope that we could never imagine without the miracle that He sent us when He sent Jesus. This is a hope that will never leave us. It is a hope that actually redeems us.

A Prayer & A Promise

Dear Lord, I know that You were with Job when he was facing the trials he endured and the sorrow that most would have never been able to endure. You never left him. I believe you comforted him even when he couldn't feel the comforting. I believe that you strengthened him when he was losing all hope. And, I know, from my own experience, that YOU are always there to bring me through the worst that comes. When I have felt like I couldn't make it down another road, I turned to You and realized that I hadn't faced even one inkling of the sorrow and pain You went through. Like Job, I've felt like I was hopeless, like I didn't have a chance . . . but, thanks to You and the love You bring to me when I'm feeling the worst, I can cling to the hem of Your garment and remember that, whatever comes, You are with me. You will comfort and heal and fill me with Your strength. Thank You, Lord, for blessing me in so many ways that I know I've failed to give thanks for the most of what You've been and done. Thanks to You, Lord, I know that I can make it down that dark road because You are just around the bend in the road. You shine Your light on me, a light far brighter than the morning sun.

> The sudden disappointment of a hope leaves a scar which the ultimate fulfillment of that hope never entirely removes.
> —Thomas Hardy

Day Seventeen

Romans 8:25 But if we hope for that we see not,
then do we with patience wait for it.

T hings I don't see that have blessed me include my love, my hope, my dream—the prayer that speaks for me, the beautiful in believing, the wonder that completes me. It is in those very things that I can't see that I often find the greatest victory. Even though I can't see a feeling, there are so many feelings that have blessed and expressed the love that silences my worst worries. Even though I can't see the future, I know it is there that I have a hope beyond every hope, a hope for perfection, for paradise, for the blessing of a love far surer, far greater, far more beautiful than anything that has ever amazed me before.

Thanks to grace, I have a hope that is more wonderful than any other. My hope is placed in the Son who erased all my worries and fears, silenced every trouble and doubt, reassured me that with Him, I'd find the way out of the darkness, the storm, the devastation. Thanks to the One I call Jesus I know what it is to hope beyond hope, to believe in a hope that I cannot see, a hope that lives in my spirit, a hope that surrounds me with grace that awakens all my greatest blessings. Thanks to His giving me a hope that promises to bring me through the worst that comes into this life, I know of a life that is forever, eternal, evermore . . . thanks to that knowledge, I can never stop breathing silent praise for the One who made a way out of the past, out of the sin, out of the cruelest places I've ever been.

He is my answer when I don't even have the question on my lips. Because I know Him as the light of my world, the joy in my heart, the hope for tomorrow, I know the meaning of love that sweetens my entire being. Because of Him, His grace and mercy, the hope that I can someday live with Him in paradise, I know what it feels like to see those things that my eyes cannot see.

Because of Him, I see the road leading me home, a road of faith, believing, grace—a road past the doubts, the darkness, the despair. On a road of victory I find my way past fears and tears, troubles that haunt and taunt, struggles that feel like they will never leave me alone. On this gentle road to freedom with Him, I am inspired to give back small pieces of the love that He has given me. As I turn each bend in the road, I find my heart remembering the moment when I trusted Him and He freed me from the sin that had brought me into a despair where I felt the grief of being without a prayer, without a joy, without a hope for the moment when love would overpower the pain and leave me with a sense of peace. This peace I craved would be the first thing to amaze me with its gentleness when I sought Him with my whole heart, when I found Him waiting at the door of my heart, when I opened up and allowed Him to take up residence in this place where I had felt the most inadequate. Thanks to His Holy Spirit residing inside, I have a HOPE that I cannot see and a HOPE that brings me real freedom and victory.

A Prayer & A Promise

Dear Lord, It was You who silenced the fears and tears that left me with only despair. It was You who filled me with faith and peace that whispered grace through my spirit. It was You who left me assured that I have a hope that will, one day, take me home to heaven where You're waiting for me, where You're always interceding for me, where You've made a way for me. Thanks to the HOPE that You stirred inside my soul, I never have to worry about my future.

My future is with You, the One who makes me whole, the One who knows my heart and soul, the ONE who is light to my world. Thanks to You, precious Savior, I know the meaning of having a hope that will never fail, a hope that I cannot see but a hope that is always with me. Thanks to You, this hope will eventually take me from this world into forever with You, the meaning of my life, the reason I survive, the beautiful that lives inside because I have YOU to see me through. Thank You, Lord, for this hope that gives me a reason to keep pressing on.

> Hope is definitely not the same thing as optimism. It is not the conviction that something will turn out well, but the certainty that something makes sense, regardless of how it turns out.
> —Vaclav Havel

Day Eighteen

Psalms 147:11 The LORD taketh pleasure in them that
fear him, in those that hope in his mercy.

R everential fear, being humble before Him, showing re-
spect for Him, being in awe of Him . . . this is the fear
that we should experience when we think of "the fear
of the Lord." Fearing God doesn't mean that we cower in fear the
way we might cower beneath the hand of a violent abuser. No, God
doesn't want us to be terrorized. He doesn't bully us into submis-
sion. He doesn't expect us to be scared to death, feel threatened
and intimidated, or like we don't have the hope of Him listening
when we pray. God only wants us to fear Him in a way that means
we are respectful of His great mercy toward us and we hope to give
Him the admiration and reverence He so greatly deserves.

There have been times when I trembled with fear of the
Lord—because I knew I deserved His judgement. I knew that I
had sinned and that sin brought me to a place of conviction that
caused me to wonder if He could possibly forgive me for this, my
great wickedness. I knew, deep down, that what I deserved was far
worse than what He would give me. Thanks to His amazing grace,
His love and mercy, His kindness toward me, I could HOPE for
forgiveness that wouldn't leave me in that state of trembling for
fear. Thanks to the hope of the awesome mercy He brings to me,
I didn't ever go for long without feeling assured that, because He
lives, I can hope for blessings instead of curses. Because He lives, I

can expect His love instead of His judgement. Because He lives, I can know what it is to share a hope that is more beautiful than any hope there has ever been.

This is the hope that sustains hearts. It is the hope that abides inside those who know Him as Savior. It is the hope that remains when all else—every dream and desire, every joy and wonder, every smile and inspiration—has been shattered. Because of His great love for me, I have a hope that brings me through the worst there is, into the light of a love far more alive than the faith that lives inside me. Thanks to this hope He stirred inside me when He lived, died and came back to life, I know what it means to fear the Lord without doubting His kindness, His goodness, His compassion. Thanks to this hope, I know grace that never allows me to drown in my sorrows or fear without the knowledge that He is a good, good God and He will always bring me out of the darkness into the light of His amazing love.

Oh, yes. I fear the Lord. I most definitely fear the Lord. He is the biggest, greatest, most amazing—He is light and love and He abides in the silence and peace. He is the sustenance that delivers me from starving for need of hope that restores me to a place of joy. Thanks to Him, I know what it is to tremble from fear without trembling in a way that destroys my faith, my prayers, my hope that He will always answer. He is faithful and He is wonderful and He is the hope that silences every doubt that darkens my world. He is the hope that ends all suspicion. He is the hope that convinces me He will always be with me.

A Prayer & A Promise

Dear Lord, Thank You for showing me what it means to fear without worrying You might go away. Thanks to this love You bring when You save to the uttermost, I know that I can hope even when it seems hopeless. Because of You, I can humbly pray without fear that You will turn away. Even when I don't feel You there with me, I know that You are there. You will always be there. You will always care. Thanks to You, sweet Jesus, I know the love that makes me aware of the hope that never doubts, the hope that restores and sees the way out of the past sins—into the forever where I will always be together with the One who made a way for me to know love that is more alive than any love known to us. Because of His love, His grace, His gift of a hope that survives the test of time, I can always feel assured that His blessings will always be good. Thanks to You, precious Jesus, I know what it means to truly hope. Thank You, Lord, for You. You are the One who brings me the best truth. I love You.

> You believe that easily which you hope for earnestly.
> —Terence

Day Nineteen

2 Corinthians 1:7 And our hope of you is stedfast, knowing, that as ye are partakers of the sufferings, so shall ye be also of the consolation.

The apostle Paul definitely suffered while he was in this life. He reminds us, in this verse, that we can expect to suffer. Suffering is part of life. Despite that some might believe, as Christians, we won't have to suffer . . . this is simply untrue. Being a Christian doesn't make one immune from suffering. We will all experience our fair share of suffering. The difference in the suffering comes when we experience our suffering with the knowledge that Jesus is with us, comforting and reassuring, making a way for us to walk through the sorrows and burdens without fear of losing the hope that He gave us when He rose from the tomb.

Some of the Corinthians thought Paul was suffering too much. They thought that because Paul was suffering so much that he must not be a good apostle. They were confused about Christianity and what it means to those who believe, though. Just because I believe in Jesus and expect to escape the darkness of a place called hell doesn't mean that I will escape the present day sufferings that go along with living in this world, where everyone faces suffering at some point. I can't expect to escape the sinfulness, the shame, the sorrows of a world overcome by sin and pain. Thanks to the Lord Jesus Christ, I can overcome the world and all of its suffering.

Thanks to Him, who makes a way for me, I can suffer without giving up the hope that abides within me, the hope of forever with Him, the One who died and rose again, giving me the opportunity to always be with Him.

Suffering is just a part of life. When someone hurts me, I suffer. When the fears that cling to my heart darken my joy, I suffer. When the faith that believes so vehemently is shadowed by the doubts that arise when I see the world's worst coming into view, I suffer. Still, I reach out to Him and believe that He will comfort me and fill me with His amazing grace and peace. Thanks to the One who makes a way through this cold, dark world, even when I suffer, I still know that He is there beside me, inside me, making a plan for me to find my way out of the sorrows into brighter tomorrows. Thanks to the love of God, the beauty of salvation, the wonder of a love that will always be alive—surviving the worst that comes, I know what it means to have victory over this world and its present suffering.

I'm always writing about things like hope and love, joy and peace, beauty and grace. I always feel more alive when my pen is inspiring. But, I do know what it is to suffer greatly, to feel so lost in the sadness that I can't seem to find my smile, to reach out for His hand because, in all truth, He is the only hope I have. Thanks to Jesus, though, I always find my way through the darkness into the light that is His presence, the light that is His grace, the light that makes a way for me to shine once more with the love that is brought to life by the One who died for me. Thanks to the hope He gives me I never have to fear being left to suffer alone. He is always nearby, providing solutions for my doubts, destroying the fears and making a way out of the clouds.

A Prayer & A Promise

Dear Lord, You didn't ever say I wouldn't experience suffering in this life. Because You saved me from the hell that sought me doesn't mean that I won't know pain and sorrow, doubt and dread, failure and affliction. Because I'm saved, I have reason to praise through the worst that comes. I have reason to praise because You make a way through the suffering. You relieve me. You comfort me. You ease the pain and sorrows. You console me with the knowledge that, through whatever comes, You are with me and You will overcome the worst the world pours out for me. Thanks to You, my dear Savior, I know what it is to have a salvation that will assure me, even in the worst moments, that I have a hope only You could have stirred, a hope of forever with the ONE who created me. Thank You, Lord, for saving me.

Courage is like love; it must have hope for nourishment.
—Napoleon Bonaparte

Day Twenty

Psalms 78:7 That they might set their hope in God,
and not forget the works of God, but keep his
commandments.

H ave you ever broken one of God's commandments? I
seriously doubt that anyone gets through life without
breaking one of God's laws, either intentionally or without realizing that they're breaking a commandment. These were
the laws that Moses brought to the people of Israel all those years
ago and they're still as serious and as wise today as they were way
back then. God's laws don't go out of date. They might get placed
on a shelf with His inspired word, but they're still as relevant now
as they were when He instructed those people, HIS people, Israel.

Even though I trust God and do my best to live a Godly life, I
know that I've broken some of these laws God gave us. I don't know
how many of them I've broken and I'm not sure I always even realized what I was doing when I sinned this way, but I know I have
done so. There isn't a doubt in my mind, though, that when I asked
God to forgive me for my sins, He forgave me for all of them—not
just the ones that are most active in my mind and heart. When I
repented and turned away from my sin, He heard my plea and par-
doned me from the guilt and shame. He doesn't blame me for the
sins that have plagued me, the ones that berated me, the sins that
betrayed me as lost and living in a world that was filled with darkness and fear. Thanks to my Savior and His amazing forgiveness,

I don't need to worry about how I've sinned or the ways that I've broken God's laws. I only needed to come to Him with a repentant heart and He saved to the uttermost.

The ten commandments are a good place to look when seeking instruction for living. The words of His incredible book, the Bible, definitely provides all the instructions we could possibly hope for. In His word, I find nuggets of truth and wisdom that I would never have thought of if I hadn't struggled through my first muddling perplexities surrounding reading the scriptures. Even though, at first reading, I didn't always understand the gift I was being given—through time and effort, through continued pursuit of His gentle verses and vision, through SEEKING and searching His word for answers and understanding, I finally began to see small inklings of His truth. Finally, through time after time of reading, I found what I'd been looking for when I first reached for the Bible in hopes of comfort and relief. Finally, because He met my hopes of understanding His word with revelation and disclosure, I became ever more aware of the convicting and convincing words, the invaluable knowledge and wisdom, the hope that was to be discovered within these priceless pages. Finally, because He knew my need for understanding and my growing faith would be sustained with His insights, He gave me the sense to see through the ink into the spirit where He lights up the darkness with His advice to believers.

Yes, I hope, without giving up or giving in to the doubts that might taunt me. Thanks to this amazing Giver of life, the Creator who is God and who gave us the greatest sacrifice, I know what it is to hope beyond hope, to hope even when my mind tells me I don't have a prayer, a chance, a possibility. Even when the doubts settle into my mind, my heart and soul believe and I hope my way through, anticipating what is possible because my God is a giver and He is true to His Word. He is faithful and He brings grace when I'm so uncertain. Thanks to Him, I have a hope that is so hopeful I don't need to know the outcome because I know that HE KNOWS and with Him and through Him, all things are possible. I hope because He lives. I hope because HE IS my Savior and He is amazing.

A Prayer & A Promise

Dear Lord, Thank You for forgiving me for the many times that I've failed to live up to Your word, Your laws, Your commandments. Thank You for listening to my heart when I didn't have the words inside me to make a way through the pain and sorrow, the sin that darkened my every dream, the feelings that bled through my hopes and destroyed my plans. Thank You, Lord, for understanding when I could not understand. Thank You for Your word, Lord, for teaching me and guiding me and planting roots of faith in me that are watered and fed by the scriptures that reassure and abide with me when I can't find my way. Thank You for grace, for faith and for the hope that comes to life inside me when I'm feeling like I just can't. Thank You, Lord, for everything You've done, for all You've been, for the love and hope that silences my every doubt. I love You, Lord.

Isn't it the moment of most profound doubt that gives birth to new certainties? Perhaps hopelessness is the very soil that nourishes human hope; perhaps one could never find sense in life without first experiencing its absurdity.

—Vaclav Havel

Day Twenty-One

Jesus loves you

Ephesians 4:4 There is one body, and one Spirit, even as ye are called in one hope of your calling.

E very believer, every Christian, every follower of Jesus is a part of the ONE body of Christ. Just like the Father, the Son and the Holy Spirit are ONE, believers, too, are one body. Together, we believers make up the body of Christ, the church. He is the head of the church and we are the body. Each believer has a part in the church, a part in the body, a part in the joy and the faith and the HOPE. We are all together One body and we have a hope that goes beyond understanding. It is a hope that takes away every doubt, every fear, each tear and replaces those with the beautiful peace, the amazing grace, the wonder of a hope that flows down from the One who created us to be a part of His body.

Christians don't always realize how important they are in the church. When one person is missing from the congregation, it could be that this one person was meant to share a word, a testimony, a prayer that could have changed someone else's heart forever. Because of the one, many might be affected. Many might come to know something beautiful, some wisdom that intrigues and glorifies. A light might come on for someone that never would have dawned on them without the presence of this ONE in the flock of believers.

We may not be worthy of the love we've gained when we came to the Savior, but we are still a part of that body of Christians and what we have to give is more important than we realize. In our walk with Jesus we may have learned something important that Jesus wants us to reveal to other Christians. We might have a thought going on inside us that, when poured out to other Christians, will be the word that brings hope to the hopeless, life to lifeless, salvation to the lost and dying. It might not seem like anything worthwhile when it's playing out inside your mind, but what you have to give could be the one thing that is the most important for someone else. Listen to the still, small voice of the ONE who matters most and reply with a hope that knows He will accomplish everything He intends to in and for us. He is the ONE who makes a way through the darkness and He is the ONE who inspires our souls to call out for Him.

It may seem impossible to you, but you could be that ONE in the body of Christ who is needed for the world to be turned around. You could be the one God meant to share a powerful message, a mighty word, a great lesson. Because of you, only one in the body, there might be an uprising of Christianity that you wouldn't have imagined.

Be that one in the body of Christ that makes a difference because you remember that YOU are a part of the whole. Just like the leg or arm can't do very much alone, your testimony or thought might not touch the way it would if you listen to the word and remember that you are a part of the body of Christ. You are needed in the body and what you have to give is something that the rest of the body needs to consider. Because you are a part of the ONE BODY, you are important to the Lord. The Father, Son, and Holy Spirit are ONE. So it is with Christians. We're all together One body with Christ as head and what we have inside should be shared with our fellow believers so that we don't miss the blessing the Lord had for them or us, the blessing that always comes to those who listen to His voice.

A Prayer & A Promise

Dear Lord, You know my heart and soul. You know I don't always listen when You impress me to do something. But, I don't have a doubt that if I would always listen, I would always be much better off than I am when I don't heed your voice. Because I know that I'm a part of the body of Christ, I know that I'm at my very best—in the very best place for hearing You, when I'm with other Christians and when I'm listening for Your gentle influence. Thanks to the gift of Your love, Your kindness, Your grace and the abiding peace that decides for me that You are the answer to my every doubt . . . I am blessed even when I'm alone. But, I also know that when I demonstrate my love by encouraging others or sharing those thoughts that you've placed inside me, I am even more sure that Your blessings will fall all over my soul. Thank You, Lord, for reminding me that I'm a part of Your body and You aspire to inspire me with the presence of those other believers. Thank You, Lord, for giving me other Christians to encourage me, to share with me, to bless me so much because I know that they understand me when I say that I love YOU!

> You all know that I have been sustained throughout my life by three saving graces—my family, my friends, and a faith in the power of resilience and hope. These graces have carried me through difficult times and they have brought more joy to the good times than I ever could have imagined.
> —Elizabeth Edwards

Day Twenty-Two

1 Thessalonians 2:19 For what is our hope, or joy, or crown of rejoicing? Are not even ye in the presence of our Lord Jesus Christ at his coming?

B elievers, followers, disciples . . . those Paul led to faith, these were his crown of rejoicing, his hope and his joy. Thanks to these believers, Paul could find comfort in knowing that he had, in fact, led others to know the One who is the most beautiful, the most sacred, the most wonderful—the Savior of the world. Without a doubt, Paul was blessed by this knowledge. He was assuredly elated because he knew that he'd been able to show other Christians the path to righteousness, the course to faithfulness, the way to a grace that is better than any kindness of this world because this is a grace that comes from the One who actually created each one of us.

Paul knew the meaning of the crown of rejoicing. Do I know what this is though? Do I, in all this modern day worldliness, know the rejoicing that comes from sharing the gospel, from giving another soul the light that shines so bright I can't fail to feel inspired, from inviting a heart who is yearning to find the comfort that can't be purchased—the comfort of feeling Jesus' arms come around the soul in such a way that the only thing they can say is, "Thank You, Lord."

That is what I'm saying—Thank You, Lord. He is the light when I can't find my way through the shadows. He is the hope when everywhere I look there seems to be desperation. He is the answer when I'm not even sure of my question. He is the reason that I know what it is to believe without a doubt I will one day be welcomed into heaven where He awaits the arrival of the children who are also waiting for this final destination. He is my everything and without Him, I am, most assuredly, not anything. I can't go one day without pleading with Him for the answer, the hope, the reminder that—in spite of all the sorrows and struggling through—He is with me and He will make a way to see me through whatever I'm facing. Because He lives, I can face the present day in this world with the promise of a time when I'll never have to cry another tear. That day, there will only be praise that comes from the music inside my heart, the music that erases every darkness as He shines His light into my soul.

Paul is there today. He is living in heaven with the One who created each one of us, the One who makes life possible and gives hope to the most downhearted of us all. Paul is there praising and I believe He is still living in amazement at the beautiful he found when He found the way to His home with the Savior. Paul might have been made blind in order to see but I haven't a doubt that what he is seeing today is more brilliant, more breathtaking, more alive than anything we'll see here in this world. What Paul is seeing is eternally fulfilling, eternally uplifting, eternally loving like no love has ever been.

Thanks to the miracle of this man named Jesus, we can each one know what it is to hope for the moment when we'll meet Him there in heaven and hold the nail scarred hand that erased our sin and gave us eternal life with Him. Thanks to this man, this wonderful Savior of the world, we have the chance to enter into a relationship with Him that will never be stale or musty. It will never grow old and when we get there, where He is waiting, we'll never grow old either. In paradise, with Jesus, we'll be eternally joyful and beautiful, like the Son who gave us the opportunity to know Him so that we might always accompany Him. He truly is our hope for the crown of rejoicing that never grows old.

A Prayer & A Promise

Dear Lord, Thank You for saving me. Without You, I couldn't face the present day, the past with all it's memories of pain, the future with all its fears and worries . . . Without You, my precious Savior, I wouldn't be able to face even the thoughts that color me in doubt sometimes. Because I know You, the One who sees me through every moment, I know that I will have the strength to make it through the worst that comes. Because of You, my King, I know the future holds a hope for me that is beyond beautiful, beyond wonderful, beyond amazing. Thanks to You, Jesus, my future holds the hope of heaven where I'll live in Your presence forever, praising and so astounded that I've been given the grace that makes a way for me to enter into a relationship with the One who made a way where no way was ever known. Thanks to You, Lord, I can live forever without fear. Because of YOU, I know a love that is more alive than anything that has ever been or ever will be. This is a love that lights up the whole heart. Thank You, Lord. I love You today and forevermore.

It is difficult to say what is impossible, for the dream of yesterday is the hope of today and the reality of tomorrow.
—Robert H. Goddard

Day Twenty-Three

Romans 5:5 And hope maketh not ashamed; because
the love of God is shed abroad in our hearts by the
Holy Ghost which is given unto us.

W hen I was younger, I didn't show my love for others
in the same way I do today. I didn't shine my light
so that others could see Christ living in me. I didn't
give off the aroma of hope, the scent of peace, the fragrance of
faith. Even though I was a believer, I didn't show it. And, I'm sure
I wasn't listening to the One who saved my soul so that I showed
the world the way He had brought me from doubt to belief, from
sorrow to joy, from lost to found and from adrift in a sea of shame
to uplifted in oceans of reassurance. Even though I claimed Him as
Savior and certainly intended to make my way to heaven, I wasn't
on the road that He had paved for me with His cross. Instead of
taking up my cross and following His leading, I was still walking a
road paved by the world, a road curving through so many colors
of fear and worry that I couldn't have heard His still, small voice—
even if I'd been listening for Him.

It would be years into my adulthood before I truly listened for
His gentle whisper. Sometime soundless, after many years of igno-
rance and ignoring His tenderness, I began to hear and that hearing brought me into a relationship with Him that I never imagined
experiencing. Thanks to this relationship with my Savior, I can
honestly show a love that is beyond my own ability to love. It is

a love that He shed abroad in my heart, a love that only He could have stirred, a love that is alive and silences every doubt or worry I've ever experienced. Thanks to Him and the love that He roused within, I know a peace that is beyond description. This is a peace like I can only believe because I know that He is a miracle worker.

He surely has done a miracle inside of me. I feel a love that I didn't think I could ever feel, a love for others, a love for—even me—a love for Him that I didn't expect. This is a love that adores and accepts, a love that reassures and abides in peace, a love that frees and restores. This is a love that could only come alive inside of me because of the faith that He inspired in me, a faith—a belief—that believes in His grace, His kindness and mercy, His abiding peace, the wonder of salvation, the victory in a world that imagines only selfish ideas. Thanks to His Holy Spirit stirring up hope and love and faith and peace, thanks to Him, I can feel a love for others and for Him that I never would have been able to feel if I'd been left to my own devices. Without Him, the Spirit living within me, I wouldn't know what it is to have a relationship that truly breaks down every stronghold of sin, every fear, all the tears—so that I can see the way to abundant life, a life that He meant for me when He saved me from the sins that had made me into a enemy of my best friend, the Savior of the world, the Savior of my soul, the Savior who is so amazing—He truly is love.

Thanks to this Savior, today I show others the love He inspires inside my heart and soul. I show, through my kindness, through my understanding, through my generosity and my acceptance of them, that I love them the way the Savior loves me, with a love that is filled with grace and hope, peace and promise, the amazing that becomes a part of knowing that You truly are a Christian with a Christian's heart and a Christian's love. Thanks to this Savior who made a way for love to abide inside, there is the outpouring of love that relieves every sorrow, every heartache, every worry. Thanks to Him, His grace and the love that makes a way for us—I can give a love that I wouldn't have even had a comprehension of if He hadn't sought me out and saved me from, not just my past, but a future without this hope who breathes gentleness through my heart.

A Prayer & A Promise

Dear Lord, When others say they've been lost in sin I am sure that they can't compare to the lost that was my own lost. They couldn't possibly have been as self-destructive, as dark and dismal, as desperate as me, the woman who gave up that darkness forever because Jesus shined His light into all the darkest places inside and reminded that, because of Him, there truly is a new life. Because of YOU, my sweet Savior, I know what it is to love without conditions, to give without expectations or reservations, to understand and believe, to value this love You placed inside more than I value the many things that have blessed my life. Because of You, Jesus, I know that love is the greatest thing in life and love is the whole reason for Your amazing sacrifice.

> Love recognizes no barriers. It jumps hurdles, leaps fences, penetrates walls to arrive at its destination full of hope.
> —Maya Angelou

Day Twenty-Four

Hebrews 7:19 For the law made nothing perfect, but the bringing in of a better hope did; by the which we draw nigh unto God.

've often heard the words, 'nothing is perfect'. And, I know that is true about most things. People aren't perfect. Life isn't perfect. Even the best we know holds imperfections that we can only hope to dissolve. Yet, there is ONE who is perfect. There is One who came into the world as a perfect baby, lived a perfect life and died to be raised again, creating a perfect hope for those of us who believe in Him. Thanks to Jesus, the perfect gift, we know the way to heaven is paved with His perfection, a perfection we are incapable of.

No. We can't possibly know perfection. Yet, we do know perfection in the One who gave His life so we could someday come home to the paradise where He abides. Thanks to the grace, the faith, that He stirred to life, we have a Father who accepts us as His children and the church He will someday bring home to heaven. Thanks to Jesus, we have all the perfection we will ever need. Thanks to Him, the perfect sacrifice, we don't need to revert back to the law of Moses time.

The law from Moses time was necessary during the time but it didn't make anyone perfect. The priest who sacrificed all those sin offerings was a sinner, too. Unlike Jesus' sacrifice, the priest's sin offerings (even without blemish) couldn't be perfect enough to truly save to the uttermost. Jesus, with His perfect life, was capable of saving completely. Faith in Him brings the sinner complete redemption. When a sinner is saved by grace and gains access to the Father through the Savior, Jesus Christ, the PERFECT Savior, there is perfection that can't be described with mere words. This is a perfection that only the Savior of the world could truly illustrate. His gift to us all is a perfect love, a perfect faith, a perfect grace.. a perfect way to reach beyond this present world into the eternal where everything truly will be perfect as He is perfect.

I'm never happier than when I'm praising this Jesus who saved me from the darkness of this life and the torments of hell. Thanks to the love He whispered into my heart and soul, I feel better when I'm sharing my faith, my hope, than when I'm doing something just for myself. Thanks to the gift of His grace, His love, His peace, I know a hope that inspires me to give freely from a wellspring of love that is His gift to my spirit. Thanks to the hope He breathed into my soul, I know a love that grows and grows and grows. A love that gives without conditions or limits. A love that is the reason I can hope, without fear, that He will answer my prayers with a beautiful solution, response, reply. He will always answer me with an insight, a smile, a miracle that provides my spirit with more hope for eternity than I've ever had before.

Thanks to Jesus, I have hope that never gives up or gives in. This is a hope without end.

A Prayer & A Promise

Dear Lord, Thanks to You and Your unending grace, I know the secret to sharing in a perfect hope that never disappoints, a hope that silences every fear and worry, a hope that goes beyond what most would think of as mere hope. This hope reassures me that I can make it through all my struggles, my trials, my tears and know the eventual wonders that were brought about because You reign in heaven, where my home awaits me. Thanks to Your amazing sacrifice, your PERFECTION, Your gifts to the soul of each Christian, I know a hope that goes beyond optimism, beyond anticipation, beyond potential for the eventual. This hope is confident, positive, sure. It is bound up in a beautiful that colors my entire soul with love that You pour over and through me. Thanks to You, my amazing Jesus, the Savior of the world, I am reminded every day that I can make it because You made it and because You made it, You also made a way for me to continue to hope and believe and find solace in Your grace, the belief that I have the best reason to hope. I can hope because You rose from the grave to live in heaven with the Father who sent You to destroy sin and convince souls to agree with Him. Thank You, Lord, for saving me and sending me hope that abides within.

> Most of the important things in the world have been accomplished by people who have kept on trying when there seemed to be no hope at all.
> —Dale Carnegie

Day Twenty-Five

Psalms 71:5 For thou art my hope, O Lord GOD:
thou art my trust from my youth.

When I was a young woman I wanted a baby more than words can say. I yearned for a child like the woman in the bible yearned to touch the hem of Jesus' garment. I longed for the soft, smooth skin of an infant. I coveted other women's babies. I hungered for the warmth of a tiny body lying against my breast. I thirsted for the gentle love that would erase more than just my quest, but my deepest distress. I literally ached for a baby who I could hold and shelter, protect from the worst and give love that was just aching to become a part of a little one's world. I wanted a baby more, way more, than any words or phrases might explain. I wanted a baby way more than I had ever wanted anything.

Time passed, though, and I was still not given the experience that most other women I knew were experiencing. I felt the pangs of grief each month that came and went without the telling signs of motherhood in the near future. I cried every month as my menstrual cycle continued to remind me that I still wasn't carrying a child inside my womb. I still didn't have the hoped for answer to the prayer that never stopped being prayed from my heart—the prayer for a baby who I could love, shelter and shower with all the tenderness and affection I'd been saving up in my heart for a child.

No matter how much I prayed though, my prayers seemed to go unheard and I never felt more grieved than I did when I faced the aisle in the pharmacy that led me to believe I had a reason to buy another pregnancy test that would soon reveal the fact that— No, it wouldn't change to that beautiful blue line that meant I'd become pregnant. In fact, no matter how many pregnancy tests I wasted my money on, I couldn't will the thing into showing me a 'pregnant' result. Despite all my yearnings, all my heart's dreams, all the reasons I gave the Lord for needing a child to love and raise into adulthood—He still wasn't hearing my need because, just like the pregnancy test, He refused to give me a "Yes."

As the months continued and I remembered all the other months when I'd yearned so desperately for that baby, I became— not bitter, but better than I had been in the previous months. Thanks to the fact that I hadn't been given a "Yes" this time, I knew the meaning of patiently waiting for something that I might not claim as my own future, but something that I might know as a dream that didn't come true. Thanks to the final verdict that pronounced me as the infertile, barren woman who would go through life without that ultimate dream being realized, I can honestly say that I know what it is to be blessed by the grace that made a way for me to let go of that dream, that hope, that yearning . . . to let go and let God increase my hope, my faith, my joy.

In fact, God increased the love inside my soul to twenty fold what I might have known. So even though I wasn't given the blessing of a baby, I was given the blessing of a Savior who reminded me and continues to remind me that I have more than enough love inside to share with others who might need my kindness, my affections, my gifts of compassion—more so than any baby I might have held to my breast. I know I missed out on something special by being infertile. But, despite that one loss, I've been given the wonder that goes beyond the missing into the message of a love that is far wiser, far surer, far better than any love that I could ever have given—even to a child of my own heart, a child—a dream— that I had to give up, because in my soul, I know that God had reasons I may never know, but reasons that were surely better than any reasons I could have thought of when I thought that I had lost all hope. Thanks to Him, my hope continues on, stronger than it ever was before.

A Prayer & A Promise

Dear Lord, In my youth, I knew You would provide for me, delight me, inspire me. I knew, even when I was quite young, that I could come to You with any need, any desire, any hope. And, I knew that You would provide the answers, the promises, the reassurance. I knew that, with YOU, anything was possible. When You answer no to a prayer, though, it is sometimes hard to understand. But, in time and as life left me with so many situations and difficult miles, I came to believe that Your no was better for me than a yes that might have meant I found delight in the moment but would also mean that the lessons You needed me to learn might never be learned. Thanks to You, Lord, I believe that the hope inside me is far more precious than any other blessing. Thanks to You, Lord, my hope is for forever! Thank You, Jesus. I love You eternally. I know we'll always be together.

Hope will never be silent.
—Harvey Milk

Day Twenty-Six

Jesus loves you

Acts 27:20 And when neither sun nor stars in many days appeared, and no small tempest lay on us, all hope that we should be saved was then taken away.

In this verse, there was little chance for the ship and crew that Paul sailed with. The prospects seemed hopeless. Have you ever felt hopeless? Have you ever felt like whatever you might do or say or believe—that still, you would not succeed? Have you ever felt like you were struggling with something far bigger than your own strength, far more capable and far wiser, something that you can't even describe . . . something that puts the heart to trembling and the mind to shuddering, something that causes your entire soul to worry like you've never worried before? Have you ever been truly afraid, filled with doubt, scared beyond what your courage could dismiss? Have you ever been at the center of the storm, even if that storm wasn't literally a storm on the sea as Paul's storm was?

I have seen the storms rage and the rains pelt away at my faith, my joy and my peace. I've known what it is to be vulnerable and weak, to be susceptible to the storm's ravenous rage. I've known how it feels to be filled with fear and to tremble at the heart in such a way that nothing seems capable of calming the soul's distress. I've known the insecurities, the uncertainties, the doubts and anxieties. I've known the nightmare of panic and phobia. I've known the darkness that surrounds the spirit of the heart who feels lost in the night, like there isn't a way to walk through the alarm and overcome the concern. I've seen the raging of the storm even though I've never sailed on those waters that Paul voyaged.

Have you ever felt the storm rising from your spirit, sending fears through your feelings, bleeding doubts into your wisdoms? Have you ever known what it is to be tossed to and fro by waves of panic and terror? Have you ever fallen beneath the burdens that haunt and taunt, burdens like pain from losing someone, grief from facing the darkness of that loss, tears that pour from a soul who is lost in the sorrow? Have you ever faced your own battles and darkness? I know you have.

We who travel through this world will, most certainly, face the trials, the storms, that prevent the soul from finding the courage it needs to lay aside the fear and just believe. That is just what Paul did in his storm. He laid aside his burdens and believed. He believed in the voice, the whisper to his heart, the voice of God who told him that he would survive despite the storm's strength. Even though his storm was scary and seemed more than capable of having the victory, Paul believed God. And, God said he would overcome the challenge he was facing. He would win the battle and come out victorious. And, Paul won. Even though the challenge was daunting and the fears taunted, he won the victory. He made it through the storm that raged. He made it through to the place where he praised God, even in the storm . . . he praised the One who made a way for him.

I'm still praising because God is so amazing. I'm praising because He is faithful. He has held me, comforted me, restored me . . . more times than I can possibly count. He has made a way for me to make it through even the worst storms I've known and He has never left me or forsaken me. He has always stayed with me.

And, oh yes, I'm still praising. I'll keep on praising through the storms that await me.

A Prayer & A Promise

Dear Lord, the storms of my life have brought me so much strife. I know that You know—what I've felt, what I've known, what I've hoped. You've known my every storm and through them all, You've poured out Your grace on my soul. You've given me life when I was thinking death. You've stirred up hope when I felt like there was no way. You've made a path through the sorrow, a trail through the horror, a course through the darkness. You've brought me through every storm, every doubt, every flicker of discouragement. You've silenced my fears and breathed peace into my tears. You've been with me through everything I've faced and You've always been the sweetness that flowed through my veins. You've loved me in a way that only You could have loved me. And, I'm thankful, Lord—so thankful that You saved me. I love You and I praise You forever.

> Hope begins in the dark, the stubborn hope that if you just show up and try to do the right thing, the dawn will come. You wait and watch and work: you don't give up.
> —Anne Lamott

Day Twenty-Seven

Acts 24:15 And have hope toward God, which they themselves also allow, that there shall be a resurrection of the dead, both of the just and unjust.

I believe that everyone will be resurrected. The just, those who believe in Jesus and call on Him for salvation, will be resurrected to a future in paradise. While the lost, those who refused to believe in Jesus, will face a future in outer darkness, torment, hell.

I don't know about you, but I much prefer to be resurrected with the hope that comes to those who believe in Jesus, the Son of God, the Savior of the world. I definitely prefer living forever in paradise to living in hell without a hope of even one drop of water to quench the thirst. I know that I want to go to heaven. How about you, dear reader? Do you trust in the One who made a way for hearts and souls to reach beyond this present world into the promise of forever in His presence, eternally praising the One who created us? Are you saved to the uttermost? Do you have the hope that brings with it, the love that is eternally yours?

Paul said everyone will be resurrected, both the just and the unjust. There isn't a doubt in my mind that Paul knew what he was talking about. He knew the way to the Father. He knew the beautiful that would silence every thought of darkness. He knew what it means to love to the uttermost, with a love that defies all odds, a love that is supplied by God. Paul knew just what it meant to share in a hope that is bigger than the entire world, greater than the seas, more powerful than anything God ever gave us . . . . this is the hope for everlasting peace, always loving, always tender, always merciful, full of grace and light and love, full of the wonder that makes Christians more blessed than we could ever describe. We are blessed by the very hand of God.

We have an eternal hope, a hope that sought us out and bought us from the past that wanted to silence our prayers. We have the light of a love far more beautiful than anything else on earth. This love is the outpouring from the God who made us to be His children, the lights of this world, the Christians who show others the way into a relationship with the Father of hope. Thanks to this grace He gave us, we have a way to silence fears and tears, reach beyond the past's grasp, into a forever that awaits those who believe that He is all powerful. He is the Maker of forever and He can take us away from the sorrows into the brightest tomorrows.

As a Christian, I know that if I don't leave this earth in the rapture, I'll have to face death. Dying isn't something I look forward to but it is something that doesn't scare me the way it once would have. I don't have to be afraid when I die, because I know the very hand that placed me inside my mother's womb is the one that will silence all my fears when He takes me home to heaven where I know that I'll be with Him forever. Thanks to the faith that He gave me and the grace that saved me, I never have to worry about dying. It is through the final breath that I'll awake to the joy that never fades away, the joy that silences my past, the joy that takes me through eternity—praising the One whom I love more than I can ever say. I love Him in a way that I can't possibly explain. I love Him because He first loved me and He placed this love inside so I could someday be with Him in eternity.

Paul knew the way to paradise and he reminded us that our hope is in the One who became our sweetest sacrifice. He gave up His life so that we could know everlasting life. I can't wait to meet Him in paradise.

A Prayer & A Promise

Dear Lord, Your beauty never fades and the hope You gave me when You saved me is a hope that grows more sure, more alive, more welcoming—with each passing day. Thanks to the love that You gave me, the love that saved me, I can be certain that my hope is more than hopeful. My hope for forever with You is credible, plausible, probable. It is a hope that I can be certain of, a hope that is alive and burns out the truth in my heart. It is hope that knows there will be eternity waiting because I placed my faith in Him, the most beautiful Savior. Thanks to Jesus, I can spend paradise with the same One who made me. I am so grateful for this grace, this peace, this hope that brings me closer to Him with every passing moment. I'm thankful I'm saved. I'm grateful that He loves me in spite of my worst sins. He made a way for me even as I was wading the filth of my depravity. Thanks to Him, I can know forever with the One who makes a way for me. He is the One I love more than anything else. He is the love that gentles my heart.

> The essence of optimism is that it takes no account of the present, but it is a source of inspiration, of vitality and hope where others have resigned; it enables a man to hold his head high, to claim the future for himself and not to abandon it to his enemy.
> —Dietrich Bonhoeffer

Day Twenty-Eight

1 Peter 1:13 Wherefore gird up the loins of your mind, be sober, and hope to the end for the grace that is to be brought unto you at the revelation of Jesus Christ;

There have been so many times in my life, especially when I was young, when I placed my hope in the world's offerings—things like houses, cars and material possessions, things that certainly will never hold any meaning in the eternal. When I think of the moments of my life that I wasted on worldliness, I feel nothing but regret for the loss of those precious moments when I could have been serving the One who made a way for me to experience true joy, true love, true hope. Thanks to the One who gave me grace that I certainly didn't deserve, I have the hope of eternity with the most high, the One who created me, the One who made a way for me, the One who saved me.

When Jesus comes back I hope that I am working on the job He has for me, the job that brings someone else into a relationship with Him, the job that gives me the opportunity to be a light in another's world, a light that takes them through the dark and sparks a hope inside that will provide the opportunity to reach beyond this present moment, beyond this world, into the eternal where there is the love that is forever, the peace that is everlasting, the wonder that is our Savior. Thanks to the hope of eternity with Jesus, there isn't a day that goes by when I don't remember that the most important job I have on this earth is to show someone else the light that shines on the life who gave the ultimate sacrifice, the life who died and rose again so that I could have eternal life.

Thanks to Jesus, there is hope that when the end comes, it isn't the end. It is eternity with Him, the One who silenced the sins of the past on their quest to torture the soul, the same One who whispered love into the heart who was once hard, the One who brought light to destroy the darkness. He is the wonder of creation, the miracle, the salvation. He is the way to know true joy, true peace, true grace, true faith, true hope. He is the way to realize that this world, with all its trinkets, is meaningless. It is only through a relationship with the One who created us that we know the meaning of life. It is only through His sacrifice that we know the hope for an eternity without strife.

I place my hope in the One who did more in three days to save the creatures He had made than anything else known to mankind. Because of that cross, that gift, the sacrifice who is still alive—who is still bringing souls into a right relationship with the One who made them, the God who saved them—there is hope that is beyond our own comprehension. This hope is more promising, more expectant, more encouraging than any other hope known to the spirit. This is a hope that prevents souls from experiencing eternal torment without the One who is, not only the light of the world, but the light of all eternity.

He is the love that abides inside and He is the love that lives in paradise. He is the reason I have a hope that never lets me feel lost or alone. This hope lingers on in my soul so that I always know, when I face death, I have a much better life waiting for me. My hope isn't of this world. My hope is in eternity with the One I love and the One who loves me with a love that is out of this world.

A Prayer & A Promise

Dear Lord, forever is a long, long time. Forever is—well, forever is forever. My hope is in that forever with You, Jesus. I hope that I'll know You better, serve You better, understand You better, when I reach that home You're building for me, that home in the forever, in the heaven where You're living. I hope that I can live this life in such a way that when I get there You will say, "Welcome home, my child—my good and faithful servant." I hope that I can see You smile when You look at me. I hope that I can, somehow, someway, please You, the One who has made a way for me to reach my final destination in paradise. Thank You, Lord, for placing this hope in my heart and reminding me that Your love will not only console but consume me with a burning fire that can't be put out by the world's watered down doubts. Thank You, Lord. Just thank You. You are my life's greatest hope.

> While there's life, there's hope.
> —Marcus Tullius Cicero

Day Twenty-Nine

Jeremiah 17:7 Blessed is the man that trusteth in the
LORD, and whose hope the LORD is.

T here have been times when I trusted in things or people
instead of trusting in the Lord. I've not always heard Him
when He told me that I wasn't going in the right direction
or holding out for the perfect moment. I didn't always place all my
trust in the One who knows me better than I know myself, and so
much better than I can know anyone else. I didn't always trust the
way I should have but I did always know just where to go when I
was faced with a heavy heart, a broken and contrite spirit, a ache
that revealed the truth that reminded me—I should have listened
to the One who I'd failed to pray to when I made that decision or
believed that lie or fell into that deception. I should have listened
to the God who made me. I should have obeyed and I wouldn't
have found myself in such a mess—indeed, a mess that I'd made
with my own choices and decisions (or indecisions).

If every prayer I failed to pray could have been prayed, I
haven't a doubt that I wouldn't have gone through most of the
things that I had to go through in order to learn what I had to
learn, discover what I had to understand, realize the things that I
had failed to absorb on the first go round. Even though I failed to
pray many times—about those things, those ideas or decisions that
mattered the most, I know now that God still wasn't without grace
and sympathy toward me. He still blessed me, even during those

times when I wasn't living for Him. He never left me in the dark despite the fact that I left Him so many times and failed to return until I needed Him so much that I had to beg Him for forgiveness, repenting so desperately that the only word I could use for my situation is frantic. My impulsiveness and recklessness often led me into places that I would never have emerged from if it hadn't been for a compassionate Savior who was willing to give me one more chance, one more blessing, one more measure of His grace.

Thanks to Him, I know what it is to be loved more than I can imagine being loved. I know what it is to be shown a love that never fails, a love that is more beautiful and more devoted than any love that has ever been. Thanks to Him, I know what it is to be loved so much that I never need worry about being left in the past. He is always there and He always cares. He never lets me down and, because of His love, I never drown in my sorrows or feel like I can't face tomorrow. Thanks to the miracle who died and rose again, I can expect to share in this heaven where He awaits those who choose Him and follow Him into forever.

Yes. I am blessed because God never lies and He said—Blessed is the man that trusteth in the LORD, and whose hope the LORD is.

I am blessed and I never have to worry about the future because my future is with the One who created me and saved me and blesses me with every breath I take. Thanks to Jesus, I know what it is to be loved beyond my own understanding with a love that is stronger and more faithful than any love that has been or ever will be. Thanks to Jesus, I know the wonderful that comes from believing and accepting His grace, His love, His unending hope for everlasting life. Thanks to Jesus, I am filled with appreciation and thanksgiving. Everyday is a new chance to say, "Thank You, Lord—for everything"!

A Prayer & A Promise

Dear Lord, Thank YOU so very much for saving me and giving me the opportunity to live a life that is shared by You. Thanks to

You, Lord, I know what it is to give from my heart and soul, with a love that is inspired by Your love, a love that is alive because You loved me enough to die for me. Thanks to You, Jesus, I am a believer who is more blessed than I can possibly stress enough. I am blessed by Your kindness and grace, Your inspiration and hope, Your gentleness and joy. I am blessed to know You, the One who is more beautiful than anything I could ever imagine, the One who is light and love, the One who was sent from the Father to bring HOPE to each of us believers. Thank You, Lord—Just Thank YOU! You amaze me and I love and PRAISE YOU.

> Faith is not simply a patience that passively suffers until the storm is past. Rather, it is a spirit that bears things—with resignations, yes, but above all, with blazing, serene hope.
> —Corazon Aquino

Day Thirty

Philippians 1:20 According to my earnest expectation and my hope, that in nothing I shall be ashamed, but that with all boldness, as always, so now also Christ shall be magnified in my body, whether it be by life, or by death.

I only HOPE to be able to remain faithful, whether by life or death—like the great apostle Paul, who did indeed remain faithful in life as well as death. He was a great example for any believer to follow. He taught us, through his own life and living, that giving everything, heart and soul and body, for Jesus—to Jesus, would bring a victory like none we could possibly imagine, a victory in the eternal that only God has the power to give us. Thanks to Paul's beautiful example, we know that our hope remains in the One who gave us His all so that we would never have to face the torment of outer darkness, the misery of hades, the nightmare of a hell that is eternal for unbelievers and skeptics.

There is a part of me that feels so much sympathy for those hearts and souls who don't know Him. Without Him, I would be so very lost. I would be lost in the greatest sense of the word, but I would also be lost in my thoughts, my hopes, my dreams. Nothing would bring me peace, satisfaction, inspiration—the way that my Savior has brought those things to me. Nothing would be understood or realized. I wouldn't be assured or calm. I wouldn't know the hope that encompasses every hope that I've ever had. This is a hope that knows His sacrifice was the only thing that could have brought me out of the darkness into the light where I finally see the beautiful that surrounds me with His enormous peace. Thanks to this hope that abides inside, I know the meaning of encouragement, positivity, confidence. I know what it is to be a TRUE optimist!

So, yes, I feel sympathetic beyond sympathetic toward anyone who doesn't want to know Him—atheists and agnostics. He is the greatest love, the best friend, the reason for joy that knows no disappointment—joy that fulfills and frees, inspires and delights, amazes and reflects the wonder of wonderful. He is the most amazing Savior and I can't possibly thank Him enough for what He has done for me and everyone who believes. He provides a hope that can't be taken away by any pain or disgrace. This is a hope that is alive, silencing all doubt and reminding the believer that, through Him, there is always a way out—a way through—a way that reassures and reflects all the beauty that comes to life in those who follow Him, those whose hope is in the One who saves to the uttermost.

I've made my fair share of mistakes. I've learned from life and living that mistakes are all a part of the breathing. Without those mistakes, many times I would have left the part about healing and learning and growing in the corridors of my thoughts. Many times, if it hadn't been for the lesson, the wisdom wouldn't have taught me the meaning of growth, the meaning of progress, the meaning of advance. Thanks to those lessons, I know what it is to hope beyond the sin, the sorrow, the grieving—with a hope that abides within where it reminds me that I am loved despite where I've been. I am loved beyond the worst I've seen. I am loved with a love that knows no end. It is faithful and wise and fills up my spirit with a holiness that can only come from Him in the form of the Holy Spirit, the gift that gives hope for every moment that I touch.

It is this hope, hope like Paul had, that teaches me to believe in a way that I could never have conceived of before I knew what it is to listen to His voice, His choice, His conviction and affection, His tender love that comes to those who trust Him with their past, their present and their forever. Thanks to his hope for forever, I can be assured that He and I will always be together.

A Prayer & A Promise

Dear Lord, together is where I chose to live—together with You, my Savior, my Redeemer, the Light that shines hope through my heart and soul, through every thought, through every doubt. Thanks to You, my beloved Peace maker, I know what it means to hope without fear, to hope beyond my fear, to hope even when I am living in fear. Thanks to YOU, my amazing Savior, I know the way is paved with joy beyond my understanding, peace beyond my prayers, a beautiful that is so startling I can't even describe the way it makes me feel. I know, Lord, that with You, I have no need to worry because You take away the anxieties, the stress, the apprehension. You fill my soul with a strength that I had no comprehension of. I love You, Jesus and can never stop thanking You for the hope that came to life when You blessed my life with this faith You inspired inside me.

There is no despair so absolute as that which comes with the first moments of our first great sorrow, when we have not yet known what it is to have suffered and be healed, to have despaired and have recovered hope.
—George Eliot

Day Thirty-One

Jesus loves you

Luke 6:34 And if ye lend to them of whom ye hope to receive, what thank have ye? for sinners also lend to sinners, to receive as much again.

"How soon we forget." I've heard that statement more often than not when someone has given something—money, time or some other investment in another life—and later on, when the tables were turned (so to speak) the recipient of the gift doesn't give back to the giver the way the giver might have expected them to. The giver is often upset or irritated by the denial, but, according to God's teaching from this scripture in Luke, the giver has no right to expect anything in return for what they've given. Is it even a gift if we expect something in return? Is it truly a donation, a present or contribution—if, one day in the future, I hope to call in a favor for that gift?

No. Gaining something in return for whatever we do for another is not the lesson that our greatest teacher meant for us to learn when he told us to give. The greatest lesson, the greatest gift ever given was the gift of grace—the gift of salvation, and that is a gift that there is no possibility of recompensing. There is no way on earth that I can give God a repayment for the Savior, for His blood, for His atonement. Thanks to Jesus, I know what it means to love without conditions, to give without expectations, to hope that I can be a blessing without expecting to be blessed for my efforts.

Although I have no doubt that God blesses me over and over again with more blessings than my little heart can understand, I know that I don't have any right to assume that I'll be blessed because I've done some good deed or given some favor to a heart who I was drawn to with my tenderness. Thanks to Jesus, I know how it feels to give something of myself, from my heart and soul, from my own gifts that God has bestowed. And, I know that—when I give anything, whatever it might be, I give that with only the hope that Jesus is smiling down on me.

I don't have a right to expect a blessing because I've been a blessing. Even though I know that I've been blessed in more ways than I can count, that doesn't mean that I should ever expect to be blessed because just as surely as I've been blessed, the tables can turn for me. I might find myself in the depths of despair, struggling with some heartbreak or fear, yearning for a blessing of comfort from His spirit, my soul's greatest gift from Him. Even though I know I'm blessed and I hope to be a blessing—I simply don't have a right to expect anything in return for whatever I have done to bless someone.

The only assurance I have when I give to someone is the assurance that my light, the light He placed inside me when He ignited this fire in me, this fire for the One who made the ultimate sacrifice for me—has been passed on to someone else, some other soul in need of a touch from Jesus, my Redeemer, my Savior. Thanks to the love He placed inside me when He saved me, I know what it is to hope that I can give something of the love He placed in my heart when He made a way for me to share in His gift.

His gift to me—this hope He placed in me, is a hope that knows, without Him, without His love, I wouldn't know the meaning of giving. I wouldn't know that the words, "How soon we forget" would be words I avoid saying because I know, deep down in my soul, that nothing I could ever hope to do would outshine the sacrifice that was made for me, the same sacrifice that made a way for me, the sacrifice that I will never forget because it means that love has won for me—eternity.

A Prayer & A Promise

Dear Lord, You made a way for me. You gave me a gift that is beyond amazing. You gave me the gift that would take me out of the darkness, into a light that shines so bright the only words I can say are, "Thank You, Jesus! Thank YOU!. You've been the inspiration, the dream, the faith and grace. You've been the second chance, the prayer, the answer to my every need. You've taught me joy and peace, hope that always believes. Thanks to You, Lord, I know what it means to give from my heart without expectation of receiving anything in return. Thank You, Lord. Thank You! I love You completely, with all of my heart.

> I only hope that He will let me preach to those who have never heard that name Jesus. What else is worthwhile in this life? I have heard of nothing better. 'Lord, send me!'
> —Jim Elliot

Day Thirty-Two

Hebrews 6:19 Which hope we have as an anchor of the soul, both sure and stedfast, and which entereth into that within the veil;

He is my anchor. He holds me, sure and steadfast. He is the answer, the truth, the beautiful, the soothing. He is the comforter, the miracle worker, the wonderful and the music that colors my heart faithful. He makes a way for me on a path that I can't believe is waiting for me. He silences the doubts I feel and reminds me that He is always there to heal me. He reassures and reminds me that He is so very real and His freeing is more free than any thought or plan I might have. Thanks to Him, His grace and His gift of salvation, I'm freer than I've ever been and I don't ever need to look for freedom again. He is the final word, the truth and the light. He silences all doubt and takes me through the regrets of my past into a victory that means I'll face death and the grave with the promise of forever with the One who created me and saved me.

Thanks to my Savior, I know what it is to feel a complete assurance in the eternal. I feel His presence lifting away all my burdens, promising me the light that comes with every darkness, the uplifting hope that comes to life in those who believe in Him with a faith that never gives in to the doubts that long to destroy the intimacy I have with the Savior. Thanks to Him, I know a peace that surpasseth all understanding. I know a grace that could only come from the One who created me. I know a joy that is beyond wonderful. It is elated, ecstatic and exultant. It possesses a promise that makes me happy to face whatever troubles I must face with a prayer that believes—He can and will come to my aide. He will defeat all my enemies with His gentleness. He will free my heart and soul so that I know what it is to be saved to the uttermost.

This hope I have, this anchor in a sea of doubt, sheds light on my past and causes me to see through my weakest moments into the beautiful that is being created by the hand who saves, the light of this world and the love that abides forevermore. Thanks to His love, I know what it is to look back on my past with an understanding that, even in the worst of times, I was learning and growing and becoming the woman He meant for me to be. Because I knew the pain and sorrow, I can face tomorrow with the certainty that HE IS MY ANCHOR and there isn't a wind capable of destroying the love and faith He has bestowed on me. Without a doubt, His love erases my past sins and reminds me, through every dark moment, there is hope that is more alive than anything my mind might think of. Thanks to this anchor of my soul, I know what it is to believe without fear of giving up or giving in to the regrets that haunt and taunt me. I know what it is to be anchored to the hope that reassures my faith, silences my doubts and restores me with hope that never lets me go past the promise that He made me when He saved me.

I don't know how to pray some days and I don't know if He will say yes to the prayers I pray anytime. But I do know that there is One who hears what I say when I pray. He listens with the love that assures me He is the most amazing love I could ever hope to know. He listens with an ear bent to the spirit who I speak from. He listens with a kindness, a gentleness, a sincerity that only comes to those who know the Savior who is the answer to every doubt, every fear, all the tears. Thanks to this man called Jesus, I know that I'll never need to face a moment without His strength stirring the faith within to make the choice that might be hard but the choice that is meant for me. Sometimes it is the hard choices that save hearts from the darkest grief. The hard choices sometimes mean that Jesus has the first say in this life where He made a way for me to enter into eternal life.

A Prayer & A Promise

Dear Lord, You know me better than I know me so I haven't a doubt that when YOU told me, in Your word, that You are my anchor, my hope, the way to know salvation that saves forever more—You were thinking of me and all the doubts I would face, the fears and the tears, the years of struggling and questioning. Thanks to You, my anchor, I know what it means to listen to the spirit who changed me and makes a way for me to know You in ways I could never have believed without the proof in the relationship I have with You. This relationship I have with You is what sustains me and amazes me. You truly are my anchor, Jesus, and I'll never stop thanking You. I love You and I praise YOU!

What gives me the most hope every day is God's grace; knowing that his grace is going to give me the strength for whatever I face, knowing that nothing is a surprise to God.
—Rick Warren

Day Thirty-Three

2 Corinthians 10:15 Not boasting of things without our measure, that is, of other men's labours; but having hope, when your faith is increased, that we shall be enlarged by you according to our rule abundantly.

P aul had hope for the church. He hoped for her to grow, to expand the globe, to swell so big that his hope for her was brought to life. He believed so strongly that Jesus was the Savior, that Jesus was a risen Savior and that Jesus was the One who had the power to save anyone who simply comes to Him . . . Paul believed so strongly that faith was poured out through his preaching and, thanks to the working of the Holy Spirit, into the hearts and souls who heard him and believed that Jesus is the way to true peace, to true love, to true hope that never fades.

Paul was a preacher who shined his light (the light God had blessed him with) into a dark world and restored the hopes and faith of those who chose to follow Jesus and discover a life that is filled with grace and restoration, a life that is abundant, a life that is lived for One other than self. Because He lived and died and rose again, together with Him, we can shine a light into the world that doesn't come from anything we might have done but from the One who did more than we could ever imagine or expect of the Creator of the world. Thanks to His love, His light can be found inside those who believe and shine with a glow that can only be found on those who know the brilliance of His Son, Jesus, the ONE who made a way where no way was known before.

Thanks to this man called Paul, the preacher, there were many who came to know Jesus and to believe in the saving grace He offered when He died and rose again. Thanks to Paul, many who would never have heard of Jesus, came to believe and receive the ultimate gift, the gift of salvation from the darkness that comes to everyone who refuses to enter into a relationship with this man named Jesus, the Savior of the world. Paul was the preacher and thanks to his preaching of the gospel, there were untold numbers of believers who reached their destination after dying. They entered into a relationship and then, into a place called heaven where they'll forever be with the One who is the greatest love, the greatest hope, the greatest light this world, this heart, has ever imagined. Thanks to Paul, there are so many who came to the faith in Christ that would leave them without the emptiness known by lost souls. Thanks to Paul, who was filled with God's spirit, they'd discover the intimacy and fulfillment of knowing the Savior of the world, the One who makes a way through the worst storms and relieves the ache that can sometimes silence the heart's hope.

Paul was a preacher and he taught those who heard him about the One who saves souls from the darkest doubt, the worst fear, the blackest dread. Thanks to Paul, many came to the faith and were left with the hope that is more hopeful than any other hope to be found.

Because we have the hope of heaven, we never have to fear the darkness of hell. Because we love the One who made us and saved us, we never have to wonder about our soul's destiny. We have a future that is so bright that nothing on earth can compare to the glory awaiting those who know the One who lived and died and rose again—the giver of life, the sacrifice, the beloved who is Christ. I'm a Christian today because I met someone like Paul along the way—I heard the gospel and I repented. He healed me and blessed me and now, I have a beautiful destiny—WITH HIM.

A Prayer & A Promise

Dear Lord, Thanks to the preacher, I met with You. I prayed to You and I repented, believing and receiving the saving grace, the amazing peace, the forever that can only be because I know You, the love that erased my past and gave me a second chance. Because of You, dear Lord, I know what it means to be forgiven and to feel the love that is all YOU, love that is full and thriving, love that stills the fear and quiets the tear. Love this powerful and beautiful can only be found by the soul who is YOURS, the soul who knows the wonder of Your grace, the soul who is filled with Your Holy Spirit and the soul who believes that, together with You, is the best blessing God could have given us. Thank You, Jesus—for YOU. You are my everything and I love You.

> My evidence that I am saved does not lie in the fact that I preach, or that I do this or that. All my hope lies in this: that Jesus Christ came to save sinners. I am a sinner, I trust Him, then He came to save me, and I am saved.
> —Charles Spurgeon

Day Thirty-Four

1 Thessalonians 4:13 But I would not have you to be ignorant, brethren, concerning them which are asleep, that ye sorrow not, even as others which have no hope.

D eath is a big word, a huge dark, a large part of what breaks through the life and silences the hope for happiness, for peace, for joy that will not cease. Death is sad, depressing, deafening. It brings a sorrow that goes through the happiest heart and leaves it feeling this painful loss that can't even be described. Death is a joy stealer, a light killer, a hope destroyer. It is something we can't control or fully understand. It feels like someone has taken grief and placed us at its core, where there is no peace, no calm, no inspiration to listen to the songs of the spirit, the feelings within, the miracle of a life that is being lived to the uttermost quickening.

No one wants to face death. Not their own death and not the death of those they know and love. Death is like the dark to a child who is haunted by nightmares when they are trying to sleep. It takes away the courage, the strength, the smile. It lifts the inspiration and places, instead, the darkest doubt in the heart. It is a grief that can't be measured, an anguish that knows no relief, a heartache that sends stirrings of misery through the soul. Death is something that we cannot control and something that each one of us must face at some point. It is the joy stealer, the pain troubler, the ringleader of the fiercest doubt. It destroys and devastates. It weakens the strongest soul and spoils the most joyful thoughts.

Death is wise in its intent to open fresh wounds and spell out heartbreak to those who don't remember, those who don't realize, those who don't comprehend . . . it is only through death that we will meet the Savior face to face and feel the most amazing grace wash through us, a grace that relieves every sorrow we've every thought of, destroys every doubt we've ever known, heals every heart that has ever broken. Through death, we will finally feel the only true victory!

I don't look forward to the dying. When it comes for those I love, I know I will feel broken and sorrowful, lost in the emotions, the missing, the grief. I know that, when someone I love dies, I will need the Savior's touch to make it through the sadness I'm facing. When I reach the time for my own dying, for my death, I doubt I'll face it without fearing. Even though I look forward to meeting my Savior and feeling the amazing love that He shines, the love that is His life, His light . . . the love that I've yearned to feel for my entire life and the love that I've known as the only reality when I couldn't feel anything but pain in my heart, I know that I'll still feel a hesitation upon facing the end of the only life I've ever known.

Even though I want to meet Jesus, even though I'm certain He saved me, even though there isn't a doubt inside me that the grave isn't my final resting place—still, I will hesitate to meet the most amazing Creator, the very One who made me, the same One who saved me. Because it will be such a BIG DEAL—I'm almost sure I'll be somewhat timid, somewhat shy upon the first meeting with the One I intend to spend my eternity with. Because of it's bigness, it's hugeness, it's wonderful, I'll—quite carefully—bring my soul to the One who created it, with the assurance that, even though I'm timid, His blessings will fill me with a greater love than I've ever experienced. Thanks to Him, I know that I don't need to fear the future, the death that will come, because He is there, the most beautiful Son, shining His light so that every heart will be warm.

A Prayer & A Promise

Dear Lord, You know my heart and You know all my fears, all my tears, all the sorrow and worry, all the joy and faith, all the peace that gives me the assurance that You are with me forever and I am forever saved. Thank You, Lord, for making a way for me to come to You when I die, with the hope—the faith—the assurance that You will give me a home in the heavens where You are the King of Kings, the Prince of Peace, the answer to my every prayer and the reason that this love surrounds me with its inspiration, its grace. Thank You, Lord, for making a way for me to feel the promise of forever abiding in my heart, for assuring me that I have the victory because I have the One who created every living thing. Thank You, Lord, for giving me this hope that keeps me through every grief. Your love is the most beautiful thing and I carry it with me, into eternity, where I'll finally meet You, my amazing Savior. Thank You, Lord. I love You!

Faith is not simply a patience that passively suffers until the storm is past. Rather, it is a spirit that bears things
—with resignations, yes, but above all, with blazing, serene hope.
—Corazon Aquino

Day Thirty-Five

Romans 15:4 For whatsoever things were written
aforetime were written for our learning, that we
through patience and comfort of the scriptures might
have hope.

J ust like we can learn from our own past, our former, our erstwhile . . . we can learn from the Old Testament. Just because Jesus came and died and rose again, it doesn't erase the former things. We still have so much to learn from the Old Testament, those 39 books that brought us such amazing and beautiful insights and inspirations. Even though we have the gospel in the New Testament to refer to now, that doesn't erase the earlier books of the bible, the ones that teach us about the light and love from the Father of all, the Creator God, the One who overshadows every doubt and reassures us that, through His love, there is a way out of the darkness. And, once we're living beneath the light of His love, there is nothing on earth that can take away the wonder that He gives to us when He comes to live in us.

Yes, oh YES . . . the gospel is so beautiful, so inspiring, so wonderful. It shares with us a grace that abounds so brilliantly that we'll never want to put His word down. With the truth of the gospel He brought us a plan for salvation that will forever remain, a plan that will save the most lost of us, a plan that will provide a way when there is no way, a light when there is only darkness, a hope when everywhere we look there is only hopelessness. Thanks to His plan, the plan revealed in the New Testament, we can always be sure that there is a forgiveness that silences every despair and makes us fully aware that love this alive is love that will survive throughout all time. Thanks to Jesus, we are forever saved and we never need to worry about dying because when we meet death, we meet the One who created us, died for us and saved us so that we will always live in the presence of such amazing love that we'll never feel even an inkling of hurt. Through Him and His love, we have the key to everlasting life and a everlasting life that is without any strife, a everlasting life that is alive with kindness and love thanks to His sacrifice.

Yes, oh YES, we need the gospel. It is rich with hope and faith and love that is beyond amazing. But, just as Paul reminds us with this scripture . . . the Old Testament still has value and we can only see it's worth if we take time to read it.

Many modern day Christians fail to appeal to the Old Testament for its teachings, but it is there that we can discover some of God's most important reminders and meanings. Through all those Old Testament people like King David and Ruth and Abraham we learn more than our hearts can take in . . . from the same people who were, like us, mere sinners. They were not without sin, but they were still priceless teachers for those of us who want to know God and know Him in all His brilliance. Thanks to the Old Testament, I can find attributes of my Creator that I might never have noticed if I had failed to venture into those old books of the Bible. Thanks to the Old Testament, I know qualities of God that I might have left out of my belief and, therefore, lost a part of the knowing that helps me to see Him in all of His glory.

Yes, oh YES, I need the New Testament and all of its truth. But, still, I need to read the books that brought God's people through so many struggles and taught each one of us so many lessons and messages. The Old Testament never fails to reveal to me the heart of a Creator who did everything in His power to save me.

A Prayer & A Promise

Dear Lord, Thank You for giving me Your word to show me how to go, how to hear, how to believe in a Jesus who remains Your heart's most amazing gift to us sinners. Thanks to You and Your gift to us, I can be certain that, one of these days, You will allow me into Your home where I'll forever serve and love You, the One who made the way for me to know love. Thanks to You, my heart is filled with gratitude toward You. I love You and I know that I will forever be grateful for the love You gave me, the love who saved me. Thank You, Lord, for everything. Please don't ever let me go—You're the love that is leading me on. You're the love that makes me whole.

> While there's life, there's hope.
> —Marcus Tullius Cicero

Day Thirty-Six

Jesus loves you

Hebrews 6:18 That by two immutable things, in which it was impossible for God to lie, we might have a strong consolation, who have fled for refuge to lay hold upon the hope set before us.

And, I KNOW that God never lies. This scripture assures me that it is impossible for God to lie. He will not and cannot lie. He is the truth and He is the way and He is the life. His word never lies. His love never lies. His light never lies. He is the absolute, amazing truth. His love shines so brightly, through the struggles and the pain, amid the pouring down rain—that there is a hope that is beyond our understanding, a hope that is like light pouring in from the spirit's candle. This truth that comes to us from the very One who created us is alive. It inspires. It silences every fear and erases every tear. It will shine bright, through our hearts, through our lives, through our worries and our doubts, reflecting all the wonder of a miracle we know as our Savior. He is the One who is so amazing that His love, His sacrifice, His gift to those who believe, led us from the sin filled life into a life of victory. Thanks to Jesus, we can know what it means to live life successfully, with joy and vibrancy, with a compassion that only He could have stirred up inside.

Refuge, sanctuary, shelter, protection, asylum, a haven of safety. In the sheltering arms of our Savior we can know a refuge, a safety, that is beyond description or explanation. This is a safety that only comes to the true Christian, the true believer. Because of His love, His light, His sheltering arms, I can know what it means to be given asylum from the doubts and fears, the struggles and despair, the darkness that haunts and the trouble that taunts. Because of His great love, His overwhelming kindness, the grace that is beyond describing, I can be sure that hope is available for me, even when I think I have no hope at all. Thanks to Him, there is a place of hope that grows more alive and more joyful with each passing moment. It is there, in His presence, that I can know true assurance, sincere grace, real hope. Hope that is beyond my understanding. This is a hope so alive that it breathes into my life— sincerity, serenity, sensations of kindness and caring that bring me through the darkest storms into the light of heavenly warmth.

Thanks to knowing a God who is love, who is light, who is life, I feel like I can let go of my past with all its doubts, its insecurities and fears, its darkness and tears, and come to a place where I know the meaning of grace, the meaning of love, the meaning of hope that goes above and beyond the optimism that might fade. This hope holds the promise that comes from the One who shined His SON into my life and forgave me for the sins that had taken my hope and silenced my faith. Thanks to the love of a Savior who gives me forever to praise Him for His amazing grace, I know a hope that is more alive and more encouraging than any hope I might have experienced before I knew Jesus, the meaning and the reason for every hope I know, every hope and every prayer, every light that reassures my heart. Thanks to Jesus, there is an assurance that my life has meaning now, meaning that it never would have had without Him, the most beautiful friend I've ever known.

Before I knew the hope that comes from believing in Jesus, I was estranged from the joy that embraces my spirit now that I can feel Him with me. Before I realized that He is the reason for my life, I wasn't filled with the light that inspires me to shine into another's life—this joy, this grace, this peace, this hope that knows He is the answer to my every worry. He is the reason that I can experience glory. He is the hope that brings me through every trouble and I'm so thankful that I met Him and believed Him, the One who my soul sings 'believe' for.

A Prayer & A Promise

Dear Lord, I don't know how to thank You for giving me this hope, this faith, this amazing grace. I don't have words to reveal the way that You make me feel. This is a feeling so real, so right, so revealing that I can only say, dear Lord, I praise You. You amaze me. You are the hope that carries me through the darkest storms. You are the hope that lives in me when all hope is gone. You are the hope that leaves me certain I can find a way through the darkness. You are the hope that means "it's all worth it" when everywhere I turn I'm seeing others let go of their dreams and let go of their faith, fall away from the grace that makes a way for my heart to sincerely say, I love YOU. You are my everything and I HOPE I can always find a way to praise You with all my heart and soul, with praise that silences every sorrow.

Hope is the thing with feathers that perches in the soul—and sings the tunes without the words—and never stops at all.
—Emily Dickinson

Day Thirty-Seven

Psalms 71:14 But I will hope continually, and will yet
praise thee more and more.

When I was a young woman I didn't spend nearly as much time praising as I did praying for what I wanted or hoped for. I was, most assuredly, quite selfish and it would be many years before I found my way from that selfishness into a better place called selflessness. And, still today, I continue to grow in that characteristic that can only become realized by the God who made me and continues to grow and change me into someone worthwhile, someone worthy. Although I don't believe I'll be truly changed until I reach that heavenly home where He awaits, I haven't a doubt that He is working on me, day by day, and I can see some significant changes in the woman who is today compared to the woman I was way back then, way back when I prayed mostly for what I wanted for myself.

After so many years of lessons I've found that I still sometimes pray for what I hope for but, instead of hearing that selfish plea coming from my heart, today—many times I hear the praise that fills my spirit. Whenever I think of Him, which is most of the time, I praise Him and when I praise Him, I am certain that I am being less selfish than the woman who, at one time, prayed selfishly for whatever her heart desired. Thankfully, I've found myself going from praying to praising and, with that being said, I've learned that, through praising, I have carved out a path to Him, my Savior, my Creator, my LIFE. Thanks to this praise that leaves me sure that I'm stirring His light so that it is poured out across my soul and life, I feel like I'm reaching beyond the prayer into the spirit who so tenderly made me.

Because I know what it is to praise, praise and praise some more, I also know what it is to love and be loved, to hope and believe, to accomplish more through His grace that I once thought would be possible for me. Thanks to this gift of praise I can sincerely say that I feel His love falling all over me, abiding inside of me and guiding me through every temptation and degradation. Thanks to this gift of praise, I know what it is to give without expectations, to love without conditions, to listen with—not just my ears—but my spirit. Because of Him, His great gift of love, I hear a whisper of the selflessness that He has replaced my selfishness with. Thanks to His gift of love I will forever praise without even thinking of giving up on the One who lived and died for me, a doubting sinner who would have done nothing in this life except think of what I wanted if I hadn't met the One who showed me that real love is the most amazing and wonderful joy that my heart could have ever imagined.

I wouldn't have ever known the joy of praising if I hadn't, once upon a time, met a Savior who pulled me away from the selfishness and guided me toward the selflessness and into a spirit of praise that shows God who I am living for. Thanks to Him, I will praise without end, forever and ever—praising in my heart and soul, with a spirit of love that only He could have stirred within me. If it is praise that opens up the heavens and whispers of a love that is beyond amazing, I will praise Him forever. I will praise Him for His kindness, for His grace, for His abiding peace. I will praise Him for hope, faith and love. I will praise Him with praise that silences every doubt or fear, lights up the shadows and fills my heart with tenderness. Thanks to this love, this praise is something that I will continue to present to my Savior. Thanks to Him, I have someone is more than worthy of my praise. He is worthy of my everything. I'll love Him eternally.

A Prayer & A Promise

Dear Lord, You know my heart and soul and You know that this praise is coming from a part of me that I can't silence, a part of me who yearns to give something to You, the One who is light to my heart, the One who is joy to my soul, the One who knows me better than anyone and still loves me like I'm the only one. Thanks to You, my precious Savior, I am forever grateful for a love that is alive and invites me to smile, stirs up beautiful in my life, inspires love that is forever kind. Thanks to You, my beloved, I will praise forevermore, with praises that I hope reach the heart of God and linger in the heavens where I'll someday meet with the One who saved me. Thank You, Lord—for this love that could only come from You, my everything.

> He who has faith has . . . an inward reservoir of courage, hope, confidence, calmness, and assuring trust that all will come out well—even though to the world it may appear to come out most badly.
> —B. C. Forbes

Day Thirty-Eight

1 Peter 3:15 But sanctify the Lord God in your hearts:
and be ready always to give an answer to every man
that asketh you a reason of the hope that is in you with
meekness and fear:

C. S. Lewis was a great Christian apologist. Mr. Lewis had such a strong faith that he could give more than just a reason for his faith in Jesus. He could give the atheist (as he had once been himself) answers for his belief. He could supply the one who needed to understand a reason for his hope, a hope that should provide any believer with evidence that Christ is surely who He said He was. He is the King, the Peace, the Savior of the soul and the very SON of GOD. He is also the hope that keeps me sane, gives my heart its grace and provides my soul with a reason to say—THANK YOU, GOD for the gift of salvation!

If I am asked for a reason for this hope that lives in my heart—I can honestly say that my reason is simple, so simple a child could understand it. I believe, not because I was told to believe or because I was raised to believe, but because God showed me His strength, His greatness, His kindness, His grace. God showed me a love that is indescribable, magnificent, inspiring and uplifting. This God I love so much taught me, through His gift of love, that He is the answer to every fear I might conceive. He provides shelter in the storms of my life. He reveals a serenity, a peace, that surrounds me with a beautiful I can't possibly explain away. He enlightens me and invites me to share in His promises, the promises that reassure me and console me, give me hope that is beyond hope. Because I know that He loves me and frees me and forgives me, I have a hope that lifts the weight of my sins and encourages me to never let go of the grace that saved me from an eternity without Him, the One who is my best friend.

When I tell someone about the hope I have in Jesus, I know that He is there beside me, guiding me and providing me with answers that I might never have thought of without His inspiration, His grace, His spirit lighting the way so that I can see through the darkness of my own words into the eternal where He can be heard. When I tell someone about Jesus, it is Jesus Himself who reveals the way for me to answer the doubts, reassure the fears, bless the listener with the opportunity to hear the gospel in a way that will lead them through the hopelessness that surrounds the doubter into the grace that fulfills and sustains, the hope that reminds every heart there is a reason far more beautiful, far more reassuring and far more reasonable than we can explain or explain away. Thanks to the miracle of Jesus, there is a hope that is more alive than any prayer we'll ever pray or any light we'll ever walk through. His is a light that stirs up the love in a heart and shines down a hope that is forevermore.

Thanks to Jesus, this hope that is my reason—silences my fears, erases all my tears and challenges me to listen to His wisdom throughout all my years. Thanks to this man named Jesus I have a reason to walk through the fires that burn with worries and struggles, fires that seem to live off my envy and pride, fires that make me realize—I can only put out the fire with the wonderful that is His sacrifice, His life, the life that carries me through the worst and fills me with hope for eternity. Thanks to Jesus, I have a reason to look forward to tomorrow, to the future, to forever with the One who is love.

A Prayer & A Promise

Dear Lord, You know my heart and soul. You know what I doubt and what I hope. You know the answers that will one day make me whole. Thanks to You, Jesus, I know the meaning of grace that is unending, love that blesses completely, hope that is forever promising me that—together with You, my sweetest friend—I will find the way to carry Your word to others, to inspire and to deliver the message that You give to the hearts who believe in You and yearn to see others delivered from the darkness of this doubting world. Thank You, Jesus, for a love that is forever, for a light that reflects Your presence, for a hope that silences all my fears. Thanks to You, Lord, I am blessed beyond measure. And, I will love You forever.

> Outside of the cross of Jesus Christ, there is no hope in this world. That cross and resurrection at the core of the Gospel is the only hope for humanity. Wherever you go, ask God for wisdom on how to get that Gospel in, even in the toughest situations of life.
> —Ravi Zacharias

Day Thirty-Nine

Psalms 33:18 Behold, the eye of the LORD is upon them
that fear him, upon them that hope in his mercy;

Even though I know God loves me and I know that I love God, even though I often praise Him and I completely trust in Him, even though I reverently fear Him with a fear that knows His will, His perfect will, is always the best way for me—I still find myself worrying sometimes. I know that I don't need to worry. I know that God has got my back and my front and every side of me. I know that He will make a way for me, despite whatever sorrow I have to face. I know that I have a God who is invincible, unshakable, so very capable. I know this. Still yet, I sometimes find myself worrying.

Is it because I'm not good enough, strong enough or wise enough? Is it because I have some flaw inside me that makes me live through battles within me that are needless and cause me to feel like I'm simply too flawed to call myself a Christian? Is it because I don't trust this God who has blessed me so completely? Is it because, just like every other Christian, I fail Him daily and need to call on Him at every point because the truth is that I am not good enough, strong enough or wise enough. But, I know a Savior who is all those things and so much more. I know a Savior who is the comfort, the calm, the caress of hope that abides inside me even though my worries sometimes cause me to doubt the light of Him who guides my foot and frees me from the dark, destroys all my worries and creates inside me a good, clean heart who is truly free from doubts or anxieties.

Thanks to this man named Jesus I know what it means to be sure of the outcome even though there is silence when I pray. I know what it is to fear the Lord without being afraid of where this path He's given me to walk is taking me. I know, deep down in my soul, that all is well—because I'm sure that this man named Jesus, this Savior, this Redeemer, is the answer to my every fear. Yes. I fear Him with a reverential fear. Yet, because He lives, I need never fear or worry. He truly has my best interest in mind and all I need to do is follow Him with a pure heart, a heart that believes and a heart that agrees with Him, to know that I will always come away from each challenge, each fear, each anxiety, with the knowledge that—whatever I must face, there is the answer in His amazing grace! Thanks to Jesus, I have hope that is beyond description. Thanks to Jesus, I have hope that frees me from worry and anxiety, hope that destroys darkness and fights for me with a light that guides me through the worst there is and helps me to see when my heart is shaking with fear.

I know that I will always have things to worry about. Some things may be selfish and other things may be selfless, but I am sure of one thing—whatever comes into my life, whatever doubt and whatever worry—there is someone I can turn to with the assurance that I will be ok. Whatever comes, whatever I face, I will be ok. Nothing can take away the hope that silences every worry I come to. This hope that comes from the One who saved my soul gives me courage to face the darkest moments, the worst worries, the deadliest doubt.

Thanks to this man named Jesus, I have a hope that leads me through the worry into the assurance, the beautiful, the truth that says with Him, I can make it through anything!

A Prayer & A Promise

Dear Lord, I know that I worry, needlessly, sometimes. I know that You know all about my worries and I know that, thanks to You, I can be certain that there will always be a hope for me. Your love is the most beautiful light and it reflects all the joy that comes to the heart who believes in You and agrees with You that, yes, life will have its trials, its fears, its worries, but because of YOU, my precious Savior, there is always a way through the worry. Because of You, there is a second chance, an unending grace, a calm that erases every doubt. Thanks to You, my precious Savior, I know what it is to be filled with a hope that is timeless, filled with kindness and assures my soul that it has been made whole. I love You, Jesus and can't ever thank You enough for Your love!

He is the best physician who is the most ingenious inspirer of hope.
—Samuel Taylor Coleridge

Day Forty

Isaiah 40:31—But they that wait upon the LORD shall renew their strength; they shall mount up with wings as eagles; they shall run, and not be weary; and they shall walk, and not faint.

My hope is in the Lord. He is my strength, my light, my heart and soul's inspiration and grace. He brings me light when I'm feeling the weight of darkness. He lifts me up when I'm feeling downhearted. He stirs me to believe when doubt has plagued me. He reassures my heart's dreams when I feel like I can't possibly find a way to bring the dream to reality. He whispers love into my soul when I feel like the enemy has erased my every thought of compassion and tenderness. He frees me from the spirit of confusion with the wonderful that comes from knowing He is with me. He is my hope and my strength and my devotion. He is love and He abides within me, preventing me from feeling alone, assuring me that His love is like a song to my soul, reminding me that, with Him, I will always know the joy of hope.

There have been times in my life when I've felt hopeless, like I didn't have a prayer, a chance or a reason to expect anything but pain. It has felt, to me, like futility and despair surrounded me with their clouds, blinded my spirit and darkened my feelings. It has felt like the worst has come and like nothing can possibly brighten my heart and soul. Even like the best things can't possibly erase the darkness that is living inside me. I have known sorrow and grief. I have felt the pangs of shame and guilt. I know what it is to lose my best friend and live in the loneliness that silences even the chasing winds. I have known hopelessness, YES I have.

But, I have also felt the wonder of hope that can't compare to any other hope there is. This hope for forever with the Savior is hope that leaves me speechless, astonished and filled with a gratitude that is more sure than any thanks I've ever known. I'm so very grateful to know the love that comes from the One who silences the wind, restores the light and frees the heart from its worst despair. Thanks to the One who lives to give me hope I am filled with a feeling that love can always restore. And, this hope is with me, through the worst that comes, among the bitter and through the sorrow, amid the staggering doubts and through the confusion that clouds the mind and reaches into the soul to discourage and haunt.

Thanks to this HOPE that is like a living thing to the spirit who believes in Him, this man named Jesus who created me, cares for me and colors my thoughts, my dreams, my life in hues of joy that bring me through the worst fears, the most desperate tears, the angriest years. Thanks to this HOPE He brings to me, I can be sure that my life has been saved by Him, the One who made a way for me even when I felt like I'd lost everything. Thanks to Him, this HOPE is a living, breathing thing, a hope that binds up my wounds and inspires me to believe in everlasting love, everlasting life, everlasting peace with the One who is everything to me.

A Prayer & A Promise

Dear Lord, You have sent me so much hope through Your love and peace, Your kindness and grace, Your everlasting gifts are beyond description. They give meaning to the word, Hope. They convict and convince. They heal and hearten. They shine a heavenly light into my soul where I know that YOU are with me, reminding me that, with You, all things are possible and this love You offer, this hope that silences all my sorrows, is more wonderful than any other blessing I can imagine. Thank You, Jesus, for the hope that frees me to shine Your love, Your light, into this cold, dark world. I love You, forever and always, with everlasting love.

Darkness comes. In the middle of it, the future looks blank. The temptation to quit is huge. Don't. You are in good company . . . You will argue with yourself that there is no way forward. But with God, nothing is impossible. He has more ropes and ladders and tunnels out of pits than you can conceive. Wait. Pray without ceasing. Hope.

—John Piper

Hope

Like the rustling of leaves in the autumn's wonderment,
There is a hope, alive like the color of light,
Singing to the heart, whispering to the soul—music
Flowing beneath the silence of dawn, amid the whispers
Night rising in gentling breathes, erasing the darkness
With a tenderness, affection much more alive
Than any recollection—like the stars glistening so bright

Like the serenity of laughter, soothing away doubts,
Lifting the spirit to new places,
Places where love never fades, where light is awake,
Promising the heart to give hope, HOPE so alive
It feels like a piece of kindness being poured out on the
Soul who listens and hears, His precious voice
Stilling every fear, wiping away each and every tear

Like the sunrise, flaming with embers—beautiful embers
Blazing gold and sparkling ginger, blushing rose
On seas of azure wishes, inspiring the soul to feel
Beneath the passing clouds, beliefs alive with reflections
In bold lyrics, vibrant yearnings—painting the skies
In rejoicing, burning away the worries with truth, resilient
Truth caressing the soul with a hope more alive than any hope

Like the anticipation, the promise, the HOPE
So alive it feels like the blessings . . .
Rained down from heaven, filling souls with the Holy Ghost,
The One who sings confidence through the life,
The One who gentles dreams and abides with peace
The One who arises, like the Son, who arose for everyone
Hope this courageous is a hope that lives on, forevermore

SDG